Getting Started with (

Second Edition

Create powerful automations with Gulp to improve the efficiency of your web project workflow

Travis Maynard

BIRMINGHAM - MUMBAI

Getting Started with Gulp

Second Edition

First published: January 2015

Second edition: April 2017

Production reference: 1260417

Published by Packt Publishing Ltd.
Livery Place
35 Livery Street
Birmingham
B3 2PB, UK.

ISBN 978-1-78728-373-2

www.packtpub.com

Credits

Author
Travis Maynard

Reviewer
Sugan Gopalakrishnan

Commissioning Editor
Smeet Thakkar

Acquisition Editor
Denim Pinto

Content Development Editor
Jason Pereira

Technical Editor
Rutuja Vaze

Copy Editor
Charlotte Carneiro

Project Coordinator
Sheejal Shah

Proofreader
Safis Editing

Indexer
Rekha Nair

Graphics
Jason Monteiro

Production Coordinator
Aparna Bhagat

About the Author

Travis Maynard is a software engineer who focuses on minimalism and simplicity. He is currently creating software at JazzHR to help growing companies find and hire great employees. Prior to his work at JazzHR, he designed web frameworks and user experiences at West Virginia University to serve their education and marketing efforts.

In his spare time, he actively contributes to the open source software community and occasionally writes about the Web.

I would like to thank the gulp team for creating and supporting such a great tool. It has improved the lives of many developers and made our workflows far more efficient and enjoyable. More specifically, I would like to thank the team members, Eric Schoffstall and Blaine Bublitz, for their help with code reviews and mentoring me throughout my initial writings on gulp.

The team at Packt has been essential to the success of the book, and I really appreciate all the help that they have given me.

I would also like to thank my wife, Alaina, for supporting me throughout many late nights of writing. Her reviews and suggestions undoubtedly make this book far more enjoyable to read.

Last but most certainly not least, I would like to thank you, the reader, for choosing this book as your introductory guide to gulp. I hope that it serves you well, and what you learn will benefit you for many years to come.

About the Reviewer

Sugan Gopalakrishnan is an Associate Lead at Nagarro Pvt. Ltd, where he is a technical lead for multiple web applications. He has vast experience working on mobile and web applications while working for a wide range of companies, from start-ups to global brands. When he is not building software, he is either reading a book, or travelling, or doing both.

www.PacktPub.com

For support files and downloads related to your book, please visit www.PacktPub.com.

Did you know that Packt offers eBook versions of every book published, with PDF and ePub files available? You can upgrade to the eBook version at www.PacktPub.com and as a print book customer, you are entitled to a discount on the eBook copy. Get in touch with us at service@packtpub.com for more details.

At www.PacktPub.com, you can also read a collection of free technical articles, sign up for a range of free newsletters and receive exclusive discounts and offers on Packt books and eBooks.

https://www.packtpub.com/mapt

Get the most in-demand software skills with Mapt. Mapt gives you full access to all Packt books and video courses, as well as industry-leading tools to help you plan your personal development and advance your career.

Why subscribe?

- Fully searchable across every book published by Packt
- Copy and paste, print, and bookmark content
- On demand and accessible via a web browser

Customer Feedback

Thanks for purchasing this Packt book. At Packt, quality is at the heart of our editorial process. To help us improve, please leave us an honest review on this book's Amazon page at `https://www.amazon.com/dp/1787283739`.

If you'd like to join our team of regular reviewers, you can e-mail us at `customerreviews@packtpub.com`. We award our regular reviewers with free eBooks

Table of Contents

Preface

I wrote this book to provide developers with a simple and inviting way to learn about Gulp and the tools that are required to use it. My goal is to keep the content simple and remain aware of the intimidation that I experienced while learning Gulp myself. With this in mind, I wanted to create content that wouldn't assume too much from beginners, while maintaining a steady pace to keep even experienced readers engaged.

What this book covers

Chapter 1, *Introducing Gulp,* focuses on helping you understand the languages and tools that you will use. You will learn how to use Gulp to perform automated tasks for your development workflow.

Chapter 2, *Getting Started,* deals with getting your local environment set up by installing any software that is needed to move forward. You will learn how to use a command-line interface and take a look at the anatomy of a gulpfile.

Chapter 3, *Understanding the Basics of Gulp,* explains the basics of Gulp and how its various methods interact with one another to create a gulpfile. You will learn how to use npm to install plugins and prepare yourself with the necessary knowledge to write your own tasks and gulpfile.

Chapter 4, *Performing Tasks with Gulp,* demonstrates how to create a set of base tasks for handling common workflow processes such as concatenating, minifying, and pre-processing your files.

Chapter 5, *Creating Advanced Tasks,* explores ways to improve our gulpfile by introducing new tasks and modifying our previous tasks to be more robust. This chapter also covers when and why to use Node.js modules instead of Gulp plugins. You will learn how to create various tasks that will run a static server, sync your project files with your browser(s), and implement Browserify and Babel to take advantage of the latest JavaScript features.

Chapter 6, *Tips, Tricks, and Resolving Issues,* covers how to improve your tasks by adding better error handling, ordering your source files, and cleaning up your compiled code. Additionally, you will learn how to set up task dependencies, generate source maps, use an external config file, and even leverage Babel so that you can begin writing your gulpfiles using ES2015.

What you need for this book

To follow along with this book, you will need to have a computer running macOS, Linux, or Windows and a code editor such as Atom or Sublime Text. You should also have a basic understanding of how to build websites using HTML, CSS, and JavaScript. This book will build on top of those skills and teach you ways to use them to improve your development workflow.

Who this book is for

This book is targeted toward developers who are new to build systems and task runners, but have had prior experience with web development and have basic knowledge of HTML, CSS, and JavaScript. It will guide you through the process of using Gulp to automate several common development tasks so that you can be more efficient and focus on what is most important, writing great code!

Conventions

In this book, you will find a number of text styles that distinguish between different kinds of information. Here are some examples of these styles and an explanation of their meaning.

Code words in text, database table names, folder names, filenames, file extensions, pathnames, dummy URLs, user input, and Twitter handles are shown as follows: "Flags are optional and are preceded by a double dash like so: `--flag`."

A block of code is set as follows:

```
var gulp = require('gulp');
var concat = require('gulp-concat');
var myth = require('gulp-myth');
```

Any command-line input or output is written as follows:

```
travs-macbook:~ travis$
```

New terms and **important words** are shown in bold.

 Warnings or important notes appear in a box like this.

 Tips and tricks appear like this.

Reader feedback

Feedback from our readers is always welcome. Let us know what you think about this book-what you liked or disliked. Reader feedback is important for us as it helps us develop titles that you will really get the most out of.

To send us general feedback, simply e-mail feedback@packtpub.com, and mention the book's title in the subject of your message.

If there is a topic that you have expertise in and you are interested in either writing or contributing to a book, see our author guide at www.packtpub.com/authors.

Customer support

Now that you are the proud owner of a Packt book, we have a number of things to help you to get the most from your purchase.

Downloading the example code

You can download the example code files for this book from your account at http://www.packtpub.com. If you purchased this book elsewhere, you can visit http://www.packtpub.com/support and register to have the files e-mailed directly to you.

You can download the code files by following these steps:

1. Log in or register to our website using your e-mail address and password.
2. Hover the mouse pointer on the **SUPPORT** tab at the top.
3. Click on **Code Downloads & Errata**.
4. Enter the name of the book in the **Search** box.
5. Select the book for which you're looking to download the code files.
6. Choose from the drop-down menu where you purchased this book from.
7. Click on **Code Download**.

Once the file is downloaded, please make sure that you unzip or extract the folder using the latest version of:

- WinRAR / 7-Zip for Windows
- Zipeg / iZip / UnRarX for Mac
- 7-Zip / PeaZip for Linux

The code bundle for the book is also hosted on GitHub at `https://github.com/PacktPublishing/Getting-Started-with-Gulp-Second-Edition`. We also have other code bundles from our rich catalog of books and videos available at `https://github.com/PacktPublishing/`. Check them out!

Errata

Although we have taken every care to ensure the accuracy of our content, mistakes do happen. If you find a mistake in one of our books-maybe a mistake in the text or the code-we would be grateful if you could report this to us. By doing so, you can save other readers from frustration and help us improve subsequent versions of this book. If you find any errata, please report them by visiting `http://www.packtpub.com/submit-errata`, selecting your book, clicking on the **Errata Submission Form** link, and entering the details of your errata. Once your errata are verified, your submission will be accepted and the errata will be uploaded to our website or added to any list of existing errata under the Errata section of that title.

To view the previously submitted errata, go to `https://www.packtpub.com/books/content/support` and enter the name of the book in the search field. The required information will appear under the **Errata** section.

Piracy

Piracy of copyrighted material on the Internet is an ongoing problem across all media. At Packt, we take the protection of our copyright and licenses very seriously. If you come across any illegal copies of our works in any form on the Internet, please provide us with the location address or website name immediately so that we can pursue a remedy.

Please contact us at `copyright@packtpub.com` with a link to the suspected pirated material.

We appreciate your help in protecting our authors and our ability to bring you valuable content.

Questions

If you have a problem with any aspect of this book, you can contact us at `questions@packtpub.com`, and we will do our best to address the problem.

1
Introducing Gulp

Development always starts off simple. You come up with a great idea and then plan out how to build it. Quickly, you scaffold your project structure and organize everything to perfection. As you progress, your small idea starts to grow into a much larger application. You soon realize that your project has become large and unwieldy, and to remedy this, you perform a series of little mundane operations each time you modify your code to keep it small and efficient. Suddenly, all of these repetitive tasks only seem to get in your way and slow you down. You tell yourself that there must be a better way.

The good news is, you are absolutely right. The solution to this development obstacle lies in utilizing build systems. They are some of the most valuable tools in a developer's toolbox, and if you've never used one before, you're soon going to wonder how you ever worked without one.

In software development, build systems such as **Make** were initially used to compile code into executable formats for use in an operating system. However, in web development, we have a completely different set of practices and operations to contend with. Over the past few years, the growth of the Web has led to an increasing interest in using build systems to more capably handle the growing complexities of our applications and project workflows.

As developers, it is important for us to anticipate these growing complexities. We must do all that we can to improve our workflows so that we can build efficient projects that allow us to focus on what we do best, write great code.

In this book, we are going to explore Gulp, one of the most popular JavaScript build systems available today. Instead of dropping you right into the code, we will break apart the learning process into simple, understandable chunks that can be easily consumed and referenced if you get hung up at any point. All that you need to follow along is a general understanding of web development and how to write basic HTML, CSS, and JavaScript.

The first step toward using build systems is quite often viewed as the most intimidating, and understandably so. For years, I viewed the command line as a tool that was only beneficial to programmers and system administrators. I even resisted learning about Node.js because I feared the amount of time and dedication required to study it would be greater than how much I could actually benefit from it.

These feelings of intimidation and resistance are completely normal and are felt by many developers just like you. We are overwhelmingly exposed to new tools and frameworks on a daily basis. It is our responsibility as developers to evaluate these tools to determine their overall value based on the time investment required to implement them in our projects. When it comes to some tools, developers simply don't dig deep enough to identify the parts that might be useful to them.

I've come to realize that these things aren't as complicated as we sometimes make them, but many developers are still psyching themselves out before they even get started. It's important to remember that while these tools may feel quite foreign at first, they are not beyond your grasp and understanding.

What is Gulp?

Gulp is a streaming JavaScript build system built with Node.js that leverages the power of streams and code-over-configuration to automate, organize, and run development tasks very quickly and efficiently. By simply creating a small file of instructions, Gulp can perform just about any development task you can think of.

Gulp uses small, single-purpose plugins to modify and process your project files. Additionally, you can chain, or pipe, these plugins together into more complex actions with full control of the order in which those actions take place.

Gulp isn't alone though; it is built upon two of the most powerful tools available in the development industry today: Node.js and npm. These tools help Gulp perform and organize all of the wonderful things that it empowers us to do.

What is Node.js?

Node.js is a powerful JavaScript platform that is built on top of Google Chrome's JavaScript runtime engine, V8. This gives us the ability to run JavaScript outside of the browser, or in our case, on our local machine. Using Node, we now have the opportunity to write both the backend and frontend of a web application entirely in JavaScript. For the purposes of this book, we will only be using it as a means of running local tooling applications.

Node.js ships with npm, a companion package manager that facilitates the installation, storage, and creation of modular components that you can use to create applications. Together, these two tools are the engine behind how Gulp operates and organizes its plugin ecosystem.

As I mentioned in the introduction, new tools such as Node.js can bring about overwhelming thoughts or feelings of intimidation. This is especially true for those who focus entirely on the frontend side of development. However, when it comes to the frontend, often the hardest part is just convincing yourself to get started. Sometimes, all you need is a simple project that can help build your confidence. In the following chapters, this is exactly what we are going to focus on, and soon all of that intimidation will melt away.

Why use Gulp?

There are many uses for Gulp, but as a newcomer, it might be difficult for you to identify how you can use it to improve your project workflow. With the ever-growing number of tools and frameworks, it becomes difficult to set aside enough time to research and choose the right one for your project or team. To better understand the benefits of Gulp, let's identify a few of the defining reasons why to use it and what sets it apart from similar tools.

Project automation

First and foremost, the ability to automate your workflow is incredibly valuable. It brings order to the chaotic amount of tasks that need to be run throughout development.

Let's imagine that you recently developed a big application, but instead of being able to allow the necessary time to put together a proper build system, you were pressured into completing it within an incredibly short time frame.

Here's an example of this: in the past few days, your boss has been gathering feedback from users who claim that slow load times and performance issues are preventing them from getting their work done and damaging their user experience. It has become so frustrating that they have even threatened to move to another competing service if the performance doesn't improve soon.

Due to the short deadline, the sacrifices that were made during development have actually caused problems for your users and the maintenance needed to resolve those problems has now become a large burden on you and your team.

Naturally, your boss is rather upset and demands that you figure out a way to correct these issues and deliver a more performant service. Not only that, your boss also expects you to have a sustainable solution so you can provide this across all of your team's future projects as well. It's quite a burden, especially at such short notice. This is a perfect example of where Gulp can really save the day.

To deliver better load times in your application, you would need to compress your overall file sizes, optimize your images, and eliminate any unnecessary HTTP requests.

You could implement a step in your workflow to handle each of these manually, but the problem is that workflows often flow forward and backward. No one is infallible, and we all make mistakes. A big part of our job is to correct our mistakes and fix bugs, which requires us to take a step back to resolve any issues we run into during development.

If we were to plan out a step in our workflow to handle these items manually, it would become a huge burden that would most likely take up much of our time. The only practical way to handle optimizations like these is to automate them as an ongoing workflow step. Whether we are just starting, finishing up, or returning to our code to fix bugs, our optimizations will be handled for us.

While things like these should usually be part of your initial project setup, even as an afterthought, Gulp makes resolving these issues incredibly easy. Also, it will set you up with a solid base that you can include in future projects.

There are many additional tasks that we can add to our list of automations. These include tasks such as CSS preprocessing, running an HTML server, and automatically refreshing your browser window upon any changes to your code. We will be covering all of those and more in the upcoming chapters.

Streams

At the heart of Gulp is something called **streams**, and this is what sets it apart from other JavaScript build systems. Streams were originally introduced in Unix as a way to *pipe* together small, single-purpose applications to perform complex, flexible operations. Additionally, streams were created to operate on data without the need to buffer the entire file, leading to quicker processing compared to other task runners. Piping these small applications together is what is referred to as a pipechain. This is one of the core components of how we will organize and structure our tasks in Gulp.

Like Unix, Node.js has its own built-in stream module. This stream module is what Gulp uses to operate on your data and perform tasks. This allows developers to create small Gulp plugins or Node modules that perform single operations and then pipe them together with others to perform an entire chain of actions on your data. This gives you full control over how your data is processed by allowing you to customize your pipechain and specify how and in what order your data will be modified.

 You can learn more about Node.js streams on the official website at `https ://nodejs.org/api/stream.html`.

Code over config

Another reason why many developers find Gulp to be a more natural alternative to other JavaScript build systems is because the build file you create is written in code, not config. This may be a matter of personal preference, but I know that this was a fundamental reason why I chose to use Gulp over other build systems.

As I mentioned before, by learning more about Gulp, you are also learning the basics of Node.js, simply because you're writing code for a Node.js application. With a build system that uses a config file, you're missing out on the value of learning the core code syntax of the platform you are using.

Summary

In this chapter, you learned about the importance of build systems in software development and the growth of interest in their use in modern web development workflows.

As we introduce new tools, such as preprocessors and JavaScript libraries, we should have a way to properly organize those files into an efficient workflow and build them for production-ready releases.

We discussed the tools that we will be using throughout the rest of the book and how they all work together and interact with one another to provide us with a solid build system solution that we can use for our projects.

With a basic understanding of these tools and their uses, you can now begin to learn how to set up our local environment for Gulp. In the next chapter, you will learn about our command-line application, install our software, and prepare our project to begin writing code.

2
Getting Started

Before we dive into Gulp, we need to cover some basic information to make sure we get started at the right pace. The most common reason why people end up avoiding build systems such as Gulp is because they have a preconceived idea that the command line is inherently hard and complicated. I know this because I've been there myself. Once I got over my initial hesitation and decided to dedicate some time to understanding the command line, I've been a much happier developer, and I'm sure you will be too.

In addition to learning how to use the command line, we are also going to understand the installation of Node.js and npm. These two tools allow us to run Gulp and manage the Gulp plugins that we will be using in our project.

Finally, we will cover the basics of using npm, and we will use it to install Gulp. This will provide you with all of the necessary knowledge to get comfortable with using the command line to install packages.

Getting comfortable with the command line

Your computer's command line is one of the most powerful tools in your development toolset. If you've never used a command line or if you're still wondering what it even is, don't worry. We are going to take a look at some common commands and patterns that you will use to complete the rest of the book and set you up for future command line usage.

First, we need to discuss the differences between operating systems and their command-line interfaces that we will use. We are going to specifically cover two topics: Terminal on Mac/Linux and PowerShell on Windows.

Mac OS X Terminal: If you're using a Mac (or Linux), Terminal comes preinstalled as a system application. Simply search for it and run the application, and you're all set.

Windows PowerShell: Our Windows setup is a bit different in that we will use an additional application as our command-line interface. Windows PowerShell is a powerful application that will make your command-line experience much more enjoyable and consistent with the commands that we will run on Mac. Windows ships with a more basic command-line interface called Command Prompt; however, due to the differences in the syntax and added features, PowerShell is the clear choice when doing any command-line operations on Windows.

If you're running Windows 8, PowerShell comes preinstalled. However, if you're running anything below Windows 8, it will require an additional download.

You can download PowerShell by visiting the official MSDN site at `https ://msdn.microsoft.com/powershell`or by downloading the latest release from their GitHub page at `https://github.com/PowerShell/PowerShell /releases`.

Once you have your command-line interface installed and running, take a moment to understand what you see on the screen. When you first open your command line, you will most likely be greeted with something that appears completely alien to you if you haven't used one before. It should look something like this on Mac and Linux:

On Mac, the displayed text should look something like this:

```
travs-macbook:~ travis$
```

On Windows, it should look something like this:

```
PS C:\Users\Travis>
```

This is a visual reference to our current location in our filesystem. The reason why these lines are different is because these operating systems have different filesystems. The good news is that you won't have to worry much about this. The important thing is to understand what you're seeing because this will soon change as we use commands and it will also help you visualize where you are within the filesystem.

At the end of these lines, you will notice a square cursor. This cursor verifies that our command line is ready to accept commands. Every command we will use shares a common syntax that is used to run our commands and specify what we would like each command to do. The common structure of a command is as follows:

```
application action --flag arguments
```

As you can see, each parameter we use in a command is separated by a single space to separate the application from its actions, flags, and arguments.

The application is the first thing listed in each command followed by the action we would like it to perform. In some cases, the only purpose of an application is to provide an action, so the additional action parameter doesn't apply in those situations.

Next, we include any flags we would like to use. Flags are optional and are preceded by a double dash like so: `--flag`. They are used to specify additional options for the action or application.

Alternatively, many flags will also have a shorthand version that is represented by a single dash and only the first letter of the flag name. In the preceding example, our flag can be shortened into `-f`. This is a helpful shortcut that can save you many keystrokes when working with command line applications.

Finally, we list our arguments that are the custom input we provide to our application. Arguments will usually contain a name or set of names to either create or reference files depending on the application you are using.

In most cases, this order will remain consistent. As long as each parameter is separated by a single space, everything should work as expected. However, some applications require a specific order to execute the commands correctly. Be sure to check out the documentation of the application if you run into any problems.

 Most, if not all, command-line applications feature built-in help documentation in case you get stuck. To access this, simply pass in a -- help or -h flag when running the application. The documentation will be displayed right inside of your command-line application interface.

Command reference

While learning how to use the command line, it is often easy to forget the basic commands that you will need to use, so I've created this simple reference. Go over each of the standard commands that we will be using throughout the book.

We'll start off with the basics, and then I'll show you some neat shortcuts that you can use while setting up your project structure. The commands we are going to cover are ls, cd, mkdir, touch, and ni.

Listing files and folders (ls)

The ls command will allow us to see what our current directory contains. You will use this a lot to see what is inside of your folders and ensure you are in the right location in your filesystem.

For listing files and folders, use the following command:

```
ls
```

A screenshot listing files and folders is as follows:

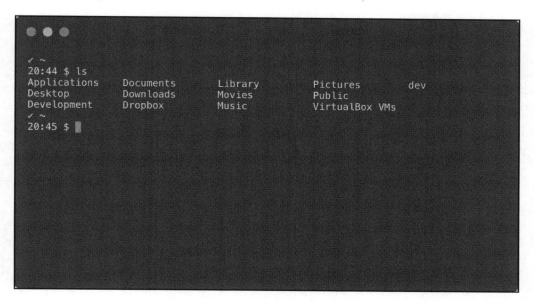

Changing directory/folder (cd)

The cd command stands for *change directory*. It allows you to navigate through your filesystem. It will accept both a path relative to the directory you are currently in and an absolute path to navigate directly to any directory in the filesystem.

The command for relative paths is as follows:

```
cd folder
```

```
cd folder/sub-folder
```

The command for an absolute path is as follows:

```
cd /users/travis/folder
```

The next screenshot demonstrates how to change directories:

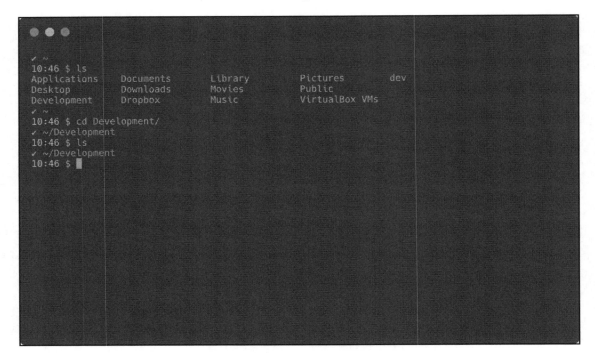

To navigate out of a folder, you simply pass in `cd  ..` in place of a path/folder. This will take you up one level in your tree.

To move up one tree level, use the following command:

```
cd ..
```

 While typing out your path or folder names, you can use the *Tab* key to autocomplete the directory names so that you don't have to type out the full path. It's a great little shortcut that can save you a lot of time when navigating around your filesystem.

Making a directory/folder (mkdir)

The `mkdir` command stands for *make directory*. It allows you to create folders. Additionally, as a shortcut, you can pass in multiple folder names separated by a single space to create multiple folders at the same time.

To create a single folder, use the following command:

```
mkdir folder-name
```

To create multiple folders, use the following command:

```
mkdir folder-one folder-one/sub-folder folder-two
```

This will create two parent folders— `folder-one` and `folder-two` while additionally creating a sub-folder within `folder-one` with a name of `sub-folder`.

The next screenshot demonstrates how to make a new folder/directory:

```
✓ ~/Development
10:45 $ ls
✓ ~/Development
10:45 $ mkdir folder-name
✓ ~/Development
10:45 $ ls
folder-name
✓ ~/Development
10:45 $ █
```

Creating a file on Mac/Linux (touch)

The `touch` command is actually used to change a file's timestamps. However, if you pass it a filename that does not exist yet, it will create a blank new file for you on Mac/Linux systems. This is why you will see it often used as a way to create new files. Like `mkdir`, you can also pass in multiple filenames separated by a single space to create multiple files at once.

For creating a file on Mac/Linux, use the following command:

```
touch my-file.html
```

For creating multiple files on Mac/Linux, use the following command:

```
touch my-file.html styles.css
```

The following screenshot demonstrates how to create a new file:

Creating a file on Windows (ni)

The `ni` command stands for *new item*. It allows you to create a new file on Windows systems using PowerShell.

For creating a file on Windows, use the following command:

```
ni my-file.html -type file
```

Unlike other commands, we are required to specify a flag with the type of item that we wish to create. When using this command, we are required to specify the type of item because `ni` can be used to create folders as well.

For the remainder of this book, we will only create folders with the `mkdir` command, but feel free to use `ni` if you are more comfortable with it.

If you do not provide the application with the flag, then it will prompt you to input the information before you can continue with the application.

Administrator permissions (sudo)

On Mac and Linux systems, you may run into permission issues as you run some of your commands, especially if the commands are used on protected areas of your filesystem. This is put in place to protect you from accidentally overwriting or deleting important files.

If you are running into these issues, it is a likely sign that you should move to an area of the filesystem where you have full ownership of the files and directories. It is suggested that you should try to avoid using `sudo` at all costs, unless you specifically understand the consequences of doing so. Understand that this section is more for informational purposes and not as a recommendation.

With that being said, in a case where you actually intend to create or modify files in protected areas, you will need to add the `sudo` keyword to the beginning of your commands.

For creating a folder with administrator permission, use the following command:

```
sudo mkdir folder-name
```

For creating a file with administrator permission, use the following command:

```
sudo touch my-file.html
```

By adding the `sudo` keyword to your commands, the system will prompt for your administrator password on the next line of your command-line application. If you enter your password correctly, the command will run with full administrator access and override any permission restrictions. Otherwise, you will receive permission errors and the command will halt.

By examining these commands, you can quickly notice the common pattern they all share. Having a familiarity with this shared pattern is great because all of the new commands we learn throughout the book will continue to follow it as well.

If you'd like to learn more about PowerShell, check out our book *Getting Started with PowerShell*: https://www.packtpub.com/networking-and-servers/getting-started-powershell.

Creating your project structure

Having learned all of these great new commands, we're now going to use them to scaffold our project folder. First, let's make sure we're all in the same starting directory. For this, use the following command:

```
cd ~
```

The ~ is a shortcut for our home directory, which has an absolute location of /Users/Username in the filesystem.

Next, we're going to list out all of the files and folders in this directory to get a quick look at what it contains and ensure we are where we want to be. For listing files and folders, use the following command:

```
ls
```

Once you've run this command, your terminal window will respond with a listing of all your files and folders inside the current directory, which is shown as follows:

```
~
20:48 $ cd ~/
~
20:48 $ ls
Applications    Documents    Library    Pictures          dev
Desktop         Downloads    Movies     Public
Development     Dropbox      Music      VirtualBox VMs
~
20:48 $
```

Next, we're going to create a new folder named `gulp-book` for our Gulp project to live in. If you would like to create this folder in another directory, now is the time to put your `cd` and `ls` commands to good use. Once you have navigated to a directory you are comfortable with, it's time to create your new project folder, which is done using the following command:

```
mkdir gulp-book
```

Once you run this command on your terminal window, a new folder named `gulp-book` will be created, which is shown as follows:

```
✓ ~
10:52 $ cd Development/
✓ ~/Development
10:52 $ ls
✓ ~/Development
10:52 $ mkdir gulp-book
✓ ~/Development
10:52 $ ls
gulp-book
✓ ~/Development
10:52 $ 
```

Next, we need to move into that directory so we can scaffold out the rest of our project structure. Instead of creating a single folder at a time, we will pass in the remaining folders we need to create all at once, which can be done using the following commands:

```
cd gulp-book
mkdir app app/js app/css app/img
```

The next screenshot shows the creation of multiple directories:

```
✓ ~
20:49 $ cd Development/
✓ ~/Development
20:50 $ mkdir gulp-book
✓ ~/Development
20:50 $ cd gulp-book
✓ ~/Development/gulp-book
20:50 $ mkdir app app/js app/css app/img
✓ ~/Development/gulp-book
20:51 $ ls
app
✓ ~/Development/gulp-book
20:51 $ cd app
✓ ~/Development/gulp-book/app
20:51 $ ls
css        img        js
✓ ~/Development/gulp-book/app
20:51 $ ▊
```

The preceding command created an app folder and three subfolders within it named css, img, and js, which we will use to store our images and source code. Next, we'll add some files. First, we'll create our index.html file.

Let's run the following command to jump back a directory so we're in the root of our project:

```
cd ../
```

To create a file using the Mac/Linux Terminal, use the following command:

```
touch index.html
```

To create a file using Windows PowerShell, use the following command:

```
ni index.html -type file
```

With the commands executed, you should now have an index.html file in the gulp-book directory. Now, let's create a gulpfile to accompany our newly created index.html file.

For creating a file on Mac/Linux Terminal, use the following command:

```
touch gulpfile.js
```

For creating a file using Windows PowerShell, use the following command:

```
ni gulpfile.js -type file
```

The following screenshot demonstrates the creation of the `gulpfile`:

A gulpfile is a set of instructions that Gulp uses to run your tasks. All the code that we will be writing for Gulp will be contained in this file. We will be coming back to this file very soon.

Hopefully, this is all starting to feel familiar. The more you use it, the more comfortable you'll be and the quicker you will be able to execute commands.

We've created some files in our base directory, but now we need to create some blank files in our app directories. Next, let's create a couple of blank CSS and JavaScript files for later use.

For Mac/Linux Terminal, use the following command:

```
touch app/css/main.css app/css/secondary.css app/js/main.js
app/js/secondary.js
```

When using Terminal, we can create multiple files at once, much like our `mkdir` command from earlier.

For Windows PowerShell, use the following commands:

```
ni app/css/main.css -type file
```

```
ni app/css/secondary.css -type file
```

```
ni app/js/main.js -type file
```

```
ni app/js/secondary.js -type file
```

Take a look at the following screenshot:

```
~/Development/gulp-book
20:52 $ touch app/css/main.css app/css/secondary.css app/js/main.js app/js/secon
dary.js
~/Development/gulp-book
20:53 $ cd app
~/Development/gulp-book/app
20:53 $ ls
css     img     js
~/Development/gulp-book/app
20:53 $ cd css
~/Development/gulp-book/app/css
20:53 $ ls
main.css         secondary.css
~/Development/gulp-book/app/css
20:53 $ cd ../js/
~/Development/gulp-book/app/js
20:53 $ ls
main.js          secondary.js
~/Development/gulp-book/app/js
20:53 $
```

If all went well, then you should be all set! Just to make sure, load your project folder into your favorite code editor or integrated development environment and examine the project tree. Your tree should look like this:

```
gulp-book/
- app/
  - css/
    - main.css
```

```
        - secondary.css
     - img/
     - js/
        - main.js
        - secondary.js
  - index.html
  - gulpfile.js
```

The next screenshot shows the tree structure in a text editor:

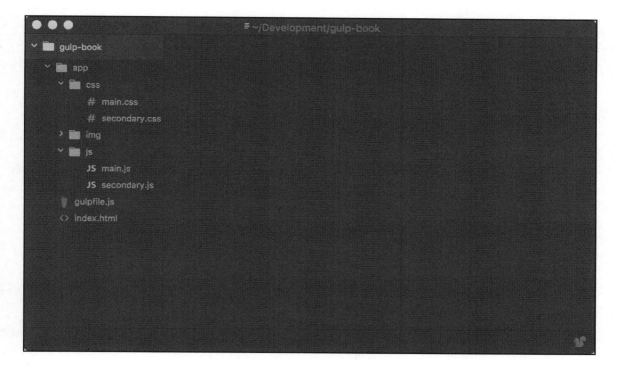

If your tree looks like this, then great! You've successfully learned how to use your command line to scaffold a basic project.

If your tree looks different, then you can take a moment to revisit the commands and try again, or you can patch up the missing files and folders in your code editor. It's up to you.

In the upcoming chapters, we will use this base project structure to build a small website in order to demonstrate Gulp's capabilities. But first, let's install the remaining software we will be using throughout the book.

Adding content to the project

After scaffolding our project folders and files, we must add code to our project. Our project is going to be a rather simple one-page HTML website. However, by setting this code up together, it will help us demonstrate the work that is taking place as we run our Gulp tasks in the upcoming chapters.

Keep in mind that these examples will be rather simple, only to reinforce those demonstrations. You are more than welcome to add in any additional code that you would like, but for the sake of simplicity and clarity, the code examples in this book are designed specifically to demonstrate the work our tasks will do to our code.

 You can download the example code files from you account at `http://www.packtpub.com` for all the Packt Publishing books you have purchased. If you purchased this book elsewhere, you can visit `http://packtpub.com/support` and register to have the files e-mailed directly to you.

Preparing our HTML file

For our `index.html` file, we just need to provide a basic structure and link it up to the distributable files in our head. The code is as follows:

```html
<!DOCTYPE html>
<html>
    <head>
        <meta charset="utf-8">
        <title>Gulp Book Project</title>
        <link rel="stylesheet" href="dist/all.css" />
    </head>
    <body>
        <div id="core">
            <div class="box">
                <img src="dist/img/gulp.png" alt="Gulp Logo"
class="gulp-logo">
                <h1>Gulp Book Example</h1>
                <p>Lorem ipsum dolor sit amet, consectetur adipisicing
elit. Fugiat atque unde doloremque illo, voluptatibus repellendus iusto,
praesentium officia necessitatibus consectetur blanditiis neque eveniet
accusamus dolorum labore iure vel, tempora odio.</p>
                <p>Lorem ipsum dolor sit amet, consectetur adipisicing
elit. Reiciendis dignissimos commodi minus sint animi itaque praesentium,
natus vel eaque, molestias sequi modi quaerat aliquam in, quisquam quos,
impedit maiores ratione!</p>
                <p>Lorem ipsum dolor sit amet, consectetur adipisicing
elit. Quos ut possimus, repellat vero modi, aliquam pariatur deserunt
```

```
voluptas quam omnis maiores eveniet quo ipsam totam quasi recusandae, rem
sit deleniti.</p>
                </div>
            </div>

            <script src="dist/all.js"></script>
        </body>
    </html>
```

Preparing our CSS

Once our HTML has been set up, we should begin writing our CSS. For the purposes of this example, we are going to keep the files rather small just to demonstrate the work that will be occurring when we run our tasks. However, if you feel comfortable up to this point, feel free to use your own code.

Let's open our `main.css` file that is located in our project's `CSS` directory. Inside this file, type or paste in the following code:

```
/* Variables */
:root {
    /* Colors */
    --red: #F05D5D;
    --green: #59C946;
    --blue: #6F7AF1;
    --white: #FFFFFF;
    --grey: #EEEEEE;
    --black: #000000;
}

body {font:300 16px sans-serif; background:var(--grey);}
```

This variable code may seem a bit unfamiliar to you, especially if you're used to another CSS preprocessor like Sass. However, the ideas are the same; only the syntax has changed. This code snippet uses new spec-compliant CSS variables to define a set of colors that we will use throughout our CSS. Because of this, we will introduce a tool in our `gulpfile` that will be able to translate these variables and further illustrate the work that Gulp will be doing.

Next, let's open our `secondary.css` file that is located in the same directory. In this file, we will add some additional styles that we will soon join together with our `gulp-concat` plugin. The code for the `secondary.css` file is as follows:

```
#header {padding:2em; background: var(--blue);}
#core {width:80%; max-width:900px; margin:0 auto;}
#footer {padding:2em; background: var(--red);}
.box {padding:2em; background:var(--white);}
.gulp-logo {width:125px; margin:0 auto; display:block;}
```

We now have two separate CSS files that set preprocessor variables and then use those variables to output colors. The task we wrote in the preceding code will ensure that both of these files will be joined together. They will then be preprocessed so that all of these new variables we created will properly be assigned to the elements where we have assigned them in our CSS.

Preparing our JavaScript

Next, we need to add some code to our JavaScript files. Again, for the sake of succinctness and clarity, we will keep these examples quite small just to demonstrate what is happening to our files when Gulp runs.

First, let's open the `main.js` file inside the js directory in our main project folder. In this file, we are going to add a line of code to just fire off some basic logs to our browser console. The code is as follows:

```
console.log("I'm logging from the main.js file.");
```

Next, let's open up the `secondary.js` file and add in another log to our browser console, which is as follows:

```
console.log("I'm logging from the secondary.js file.");
```

Our project files have now been set up to demonstrate the processing that we will be doing with gulp. We will be revisiting these files in the next chapter when we begin writing our tasks. Next, we will install the remaining software that we will use throughout the book.

Adding images

Our project will also contain some images. You are more than welcome to include any images you would like; however, if you would like to follow along with the book, I have provided some images for you in the project files for this chapter. You can download these files from Packt's website.

Summary

In this chapter, you learned about how to use a command-line application to navigate a filesystem and create new files and folders. With this newfound knowledge, we scaffolded our project directory that we will use throughout the remainder of the book. In the next chapter, we will dive into the basics of Gulp to better understand how it works in preparation for writing our own gulpfiles.

3
Understanding the Basics of Gulp

In this chapter, we will take a look at the basics of Gulp and how it works. Understanding some of the basic principles and philosophies behind the tool, it's plugin system will assist you as you begin writing your own gulpfiles. We'll start by taking a look at the engine behind Gulp and then follow up by breaking down the inner workings of Gulp itself. By the end of this chapter, you will be ready to begin writing your own gulpfile.

Installing Node.js and npm

As you learned in the introduction, Node.js and npm are the engines that work behind the scenes that allow us to operate Gulp and keep track of any plugins we decide to use.

Downloading and installing Node.js

For Mac and Windows, the installation is quite simple. All you need to do is navigate over to `http://nodejs.org` and click on the big green install button. Once the installer has finished downloading, run the application and it will install both Node.js and npm.

For Linux, there are a couple more steps, but don't worry; with your newly acquired command-line skills, it should be relatively simple. To install Node.js and npm on Linux, you'll need to run the following three commands in Terminal:

```
sudo add-apt-repository ppa:chris-lea/node.js
sudo apt-get update
sudo apt-get install nodejs
```

The details of these commands are outside the scope of this book, but just for reference, they add a repository to the list of available packages, update the total list of packages, and then install the application from the repository we added.

Verify the installation

To confirm that our installation was successful, try the following command in your command line:

```
node -v
```

If Node.js is successfully installed, node -v will output a version number on the next line of your command line. Now, let's do the same with npm:

```
npm -v
```

Like before, if your installation was successful, npm -v should output the version number of npm on the next line.

```
● ● ●
✓ ~/Development/gulp-book
16:30 $ node -v
v6.10.2
✓ ~/Development/gulp-book
16:30 $ npm -v
3.10.10
✓ ~/Development/gulp-book
16:31 $ █
```

The versions displayed in this screenshot reflect the latest **Long Term Support** (**LTS**) release currently available as of writing this. This may differ from the version that you have installed, depending on when you're reading this. It's always suggested that you use the latest LTS release when possible.

 The -v command is a common flag used by most command-line applications to quickly display their version number. This is very useful to debug version issues while using command-line applications.

Creating a package.json file

Having npm in our workflow will make installing packages incredibly easy; however, we should look ahead and establish a way to keep track of all the packages (or dependencies) that we use in our projects. Keeping track of dependencies is very important to keep your workflow consistent across development environments.

Node.js uses a file named package.json to store information about your project, and npm uses this same file to manage all of the package dependencies your project requires to run properly.

In any project using Gulp, it is always a great practice to create this file ahead of time so that you can easily populate your dependency list as you are installing packages or plugins.

To create the package.json file, we will need to run npm's built-in init action using the following command:

```
npm init
```

Now, using the preceding command, the terminal will show the following output:

```
● ● ●
  ✓ ~/Development/gulp-book
  20:56 $ npm init
  This utility will walk you through creating a package.json file.
  It only covers the most common items, and tries to guess sensible defaults.

  See `npm help json` for definitive documentation on these fields
  and exactly what they do.

  Use `npm install <pkg> --save` afterwards to install a package and
  save it as a dependency in the package.json file.

  Press ^C at any time to quit.
  name: (gulp-book) ▌
```

Your command line will prompt you several times, asking for basic information about the project, such as the project name, author, and version number. You can accept the defaults for these fields by simply pressing the *Enter* key at each prompt. Most of this information is used primarily on the npm website if a developer decides to publish a Node.js package. For our purposes, we will just use it to initialize the file so that we can properly add our dependencies as we move forward. The screenshot for the preceding command is as follows:

```
● ● ●
  git repository:
  keywords:
  author: Travis Maynard
  license: (ISC)
  About to write to /Users/travismaynard/Development/gulp-book/package.json:

  {
    "name": "gulp-book",
    "version": "1.0.0",
    "description": "A sample gulp project.",
    "main": "gulpfile.js",
    "scripts": {
      "test": "echo \"Error: no test specified\" && exit 1"
    },
    "author": "Travis Maynard",
    "license": "ISC"
  }


  Is this ok? (yes) ▌
```

Installing Gulp

With npm installed and our `package.json` file created, we are now ready to begin installing Node.js packages. The first and most important package we will install is none other than Gulp itself.

Locating Gulp

Locating and gathering information about Node.js packages is very simple, thanks to the npm registry. The npm registry is a companion website that keeps track of all the published Node.js modules, including gulp and gulp plugins. You can find this registry at `http://npmjs.org`. Take a moment to visit the npm registry and do a quick search for gulp.

The listing page for each Node.js module will give you detailed information on each project, including the author, version number, and dependencies. Additionally, it also features a small snippet of command-line code that you can use to install the package, along with readme information that will outline basic usage of the package and other useful information.

Installing gulp locally

Before we install gulp, make sure you are in your project's root directory, gulp-book, using the `cd` and `ls` commands you learned earlier. If you ever need to brush up on any of the standard commands, feel free to take a moment to step back and review as we progress through the book.

To install packages with npm, we will follow a similar pattern to the ones we've used previously. Since we will be covering both versions 3.x and 4.x in this book, we'll demonstrate installing both:

To install Gulp 3.x, you can use the following:

```
npm install --save-dev gulp
```

To install Gulp 4.x, you can use the following:

```
npm install --save-dev gulpjs/gulp#4.0
```

This command is quite different from the 3.x command, because this command is installing the latest development release directly from GitHub. Since the 4.x version is still being actively developed, this is the only way to install it at the time of writing this book. Once released, you will be able to run the previous command without installing from GitHub.

Upon executing the command, it will result in output similar to the following:

```
                  ├── lodash@1.0.2
                  └── minimatch@0.2.14
                      ├── lru-cache@2.7.3
                      └── sigmund@1.0.1
        ┬── graceful-fs@3.0.11
        └── natives@1.1.0
        ┬── mkdirp@0.5.1
        └── minimist@0.0.8
        ┬── strip-bom@1.0.0
        ├── first-chunk-stream@1.0.0
        └── is-utf8@0.2.1
        ┬── through2@0.6.5
        └┬── readable-stream@1.0.34
         └── isarray@0.0.1
        └┬── vinyl@0.4.6
         └── clone@0.2.0

npm WARN gulp-book@1.0.0 No repository field.
✓ ~/Development/gulp-book
20:58 $ █
```

To break this down, let's examine each piece of this command to better understand how npm works:

- `npm`: This is the application we are running.
- `install`: This is the action that we want the program to run. In this case, we are instructing npm to install something in our local folder.
- `--save-dev`: This is a flag that tells npm to add this module to the `dev` dependencies list in our `package.json` file.
- `gulp`: This is the package we would like to install.

 Additionally, npm has a `--save` flag, which saves the module to the list of `dependencies` instead of `devDependencies`. These dependency lists are used to separate the modules that a project depends on to run and the modules a project depends on when in development. Since we are using gulp to assist us in development, we will always use the `--save-dev` flag throughout the book.

So, this command will use npm to contact the npm registry, and it will install gulp to our local `gulp-book` directory. After using this command, you will note that a new folder has been created, which is named `node_modules`. It is where Node.js and npm store all of the installed packages and dependencies of your project. Take a look at the following screenshot:

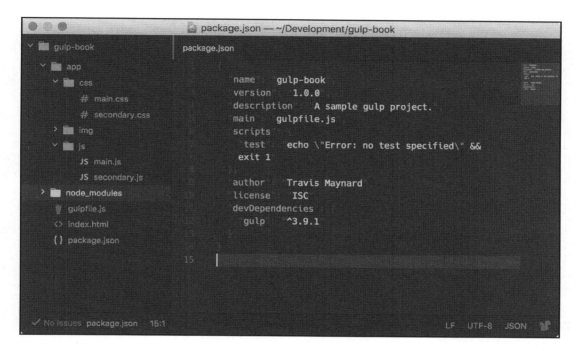

Installing gulp-cli globally

For many of the packages that we install, this will be all that is needed. With gulp, we must install a companion module `gulp-cli` globally so that we can use the gulp command from anywhere in our filesystem. To install `gulp-cli` globally, use the following command:

```
npm install -g gulp-cli
```

In this command, not much has changed compared to the original command where we installed the gulp package locally. We've only added a `-g` flag to the command, which instructs npm to install the package globally.

On Windows, your console window should be opened under an administrator account in order to install an npm package globally.

At first, this can be a little confusing, and for many packages it won't apply. Similar build systems actually separate these usages into two different packages that must be installed separately; one that is installed globally for command-line use and another installed locally in your project.

Gulp was created so that both of these usages could be combined into a single package and, based on where you install it, it could operate in different ways.

Anatomy of a gulpfile

Before we can begin writing tasks, we should take a look at the anatomy and structure of a `gulpfile`. Examining the code of a `gulpfile` will allow us to better understand what is happening as we run our tasks.

Gulp started with four main methods: `.task()`, `.src()`, `.watch()`, and `.dest()`. The release of version 4.x introduced additional methods such as `.series()` and `.parallel()`. In addition to the gulp API methods, each task will also make use of the Node.js `.pipe()` method. This small list of methods is all that is needed to understand how to begin writing basic tasks. They each represent a specific purpose and will act as the building blocks of our `gulpfile`.

The task() method

The `.task()` method is the basic wrapper for which we create our tasks. Its syntax is `.task(string, function)`. It takes two arguments—string value representing the name of the task and a function that will contain the code you wish to execute upon running that task.

The src() method

The `.src()` method is our input or how we gain access to the source files that we plan on modifying. It accepts either a single glob string or an array of glob strings as an argument. Globs are a pattern that we can use to make our paths more dynamic. When using globs, we can match an entire set of files with a single string using *wildcard* characters as opposed to listing them all separately. The syntax is for this method is `.src(string || array)`.

The watch() method

The `.watch()` method is used to specifically look for changes in our files. This will allow us to keep gulp running as we code so that we don't need to rerun gulp any time we need to process our tasks. This syntax is different between the 3.x and 4.x version.

For version 3.x, the syntax is— `.watch(string || array, array)`, with the first argument being our paths/globs to watch and the second argument being the array of task names that need to be run when those files change.

For version 4.x, the syntax has changed a bit to allow for two new methods that provide more explicit control of the order in which tasks are executed. When using 4.x, instead of passing in an array as the second argument, we will use either the `.series()` or `.parallel()` method like so— `.watch(string || array, gulp.series() || gulp.parallel())`.

The dest() method

The `dest()` method is used to set the output destination of your processed file. Most often, this will be used to output our data into a `build` or `dist` folder that will be either shared as a library or accessed by your application. The syntax for this method is `.dest(string)`.

The pipe() method

The `.pipe()` method will allow us to pipe together smaller single-purpose plugins or applications into a pipechain. This is what gives us full control of the order in which we would need to process our files. The syntax for this method is `.pipe(function)`.

The parallel() and series() methods

The parallel and series methods were added in version 4.x as a way to easily control whether your tasks are run together all at once or in a sequence one after the other. This is important if one of your tasks requires that other tasks complete before it can be run successfully. When using these methods, the arguments will be the string names of your tasks, separated by a comma. The syntax for these methods is— `.series(tasks)` and `.parallel(tasks)`.

Understanding these methods will take you far, as these are the core elements of building your tasks. Next, we will need to put these methods together and explain how they all interact with one another to create a gulp task.

Including modules/plugins

When writing a `gulpfile`, you will always start by including the modules or plugins you are going to use in your tasks. These can be both gulp plugins and Node.js modules, based on what your needs are. Gulp plugins are small Node.js applications built for use inside of gulp to provide a single-purpose action, and can be chained together to create complex operations for your data. Node.js modules serve a broader purpose and can be used with gulp or independently.

Next, we can open our `gulpfile.js` file and add the following code:

```
// Load Node Modules/Plugins
var gulp = require('gulp');
var concat = require('gulp-concat');
var uglify = require('gulp-uglify');
```

The `gulpfile.js` file will look as shown in the following screenshot:

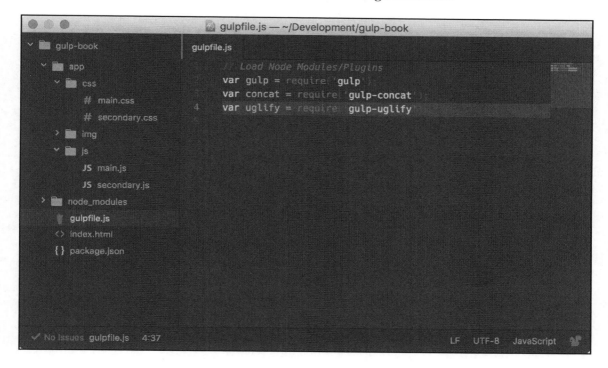

In this code, we have included gulp and two gulp plugins: `gulp-concat` and `gulp-uglify`. As you can now see, including a plugin into your `gulpfile` is quite easy. After we install each module or plugin using npm, you simply use Node.js' `require()` function and pass it in the name of the module. You then assign it to a new variable so that you can use it throughout your `gulpfile`.

This is Node.js' way of handling modularity, and because a `gulpfile` is essentially a small Node.js application, it adopts this practice as well.

Writing a task

All tasks in gulp share a common structure. Having reviewed the five methods at the beginning of this section, you will already be familiar with most of it. Some tasks might end up being larger than others, but they still follow the same pattern. To better illustrate how they work, let's examine a bare skeleton of a task. This skeleton is the basic *bone structure* of each task we will be creating. Studying this structure will make it incredibly simple to understand how parts of gulp work together to create a task. An example of a sample task is as follows:

```
gulp.task(name, function() {
    return gulp.src(path)
      .pipe(plugin)
      .pipe(plugin)
      .pipe(gulp.dest(path));
});
```

In the first line, we use the new gulp variable that we created a moment ago and access the `.task()` method. This creates a new task in our `gulpfile`. As you learned earlier, the task method accepts two arguments: a task name as a string and a callback function that will contain the actions we wish to run when this task is executed.

Inside the callback function, we reference the gulp variable once more and then use the `.src()` method to provide the input to our task. As you learned earlier, the source method accepts a path or an array of paths to the files that we wish to process.

Next, we have a series of three `.pipe()` methods. In each of these pipe methods, we will specify which plugin we would like to use. This grouping of pipes is what we call our pipechain.

The data that we have provided gulp with in our source method will flow through our pipechain to be modified by each piped plugin that it passes through. The order of the pipe methods is entirely up to you. This gives you a great deal of control over how and when your data is modified.

You may have noticed that the final pipe is a bit different. At the end of our pipechain, we have to tell gulp to move our modified file somewhere. This is where the `.dest()` method comes into play. As we mentioned earlier, the destination method accepts a path that sets the destination of the processed file as it reaches the end of our pipechain. If `.src()` is our input, then `.dest()` is our output.

Reflection

To wrap up, take a moment to look at a finished `gulpfile` and reflect on the information that we just covered. This is the completed `gulpfile` that we will be creating from scratch in the next chapter, so don't worry if you still feel lost. This is just an opportunity to recognize the patterns and syntaxes that we have been studying so far.

In the next chapter, we will begin creating this file step by step:

```javascript
// Load Node Modules/Plugins
var gulp = require('gulp');
var concat = require('gulp-concat');
var uglify = require('gulp-uglify');

// Process Styles
gulp.task('styles', function() {
    return gulp.src('css/*.css')
        .pipe(concat('all.css'))
        .pipe(gulp.dest('dist/'));
});

// Process Scripts
gulp.task('scripts', function() {
    return gulp.src('js/*.js')
        .pipe(concat('all.js'))
        .pipe(uglify())
        .pipe(gulp.dest('dist/'));
});

// Watch Files For Changes
gulp.task('watch', function() {
    gulp.watch('css/*.css', 'styles');
    gulp.watch('js/*.js', 'scripts');
});

// Default Task
gulp.task('default', gulp.parallel('styles', 'scripts', 'watch'));
```

The `gulpfile.js` file will look as follows:

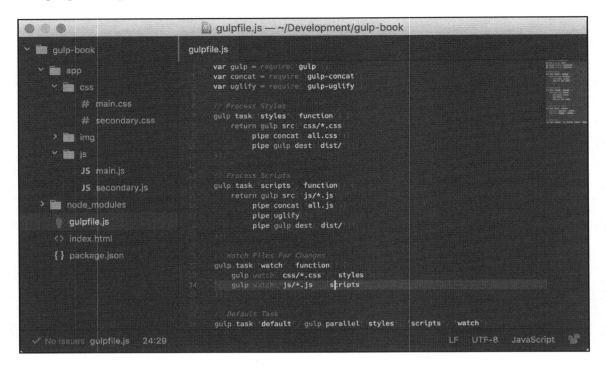

Summary

In this chapter, you installed Node.js, learned the basics of how to use npm, and understood how and why to install gulp both locally and globally. We also covered some of the core differences between the 3.x and 4.x versions of gulp and how they will affect your gulpfiles as we move forward.

To wrap up the chapter, we took a small glimpse into the anatomy of a gulpfile to prepare us for writing our own gulpfiles from scratch in the next chapter.

4
Performing Tasks with Gulp

We have spent a lot of time preparing you for this moment. It is finally time to write some code. For this simple project, we will use a very basic *Hello, world!* style examples to demonstrate how Gulp accesses, modifies, and outputs our code and images.

Our project will create separate tasks that will process CSS, JavaScript, and images. For CSS, we will combine all of the files into a single file and then preprocess it to enable additional features in our code. For JavaScript, we will combine the files, check the code for errors, and minify it to reduce the overall file size. For images, we will use a plugin to compress and optimize them so our project will load faster and more efficiently.

Using Gulp plugins

Without plugins, Gulp is simply a means of connecting and organizing small bits of functionality. The plugins we are going to install will add the functionality we need to properly modify and optimize our code. Like Gulp, all of the Gulp plugins we will be using are installed via npm.

It is important to note that the Gulp team cares deeply about their plugin ecosystem and spends a lot of time making sure they eliminate any that misuse their plugin philosophy or duplicate other plugins. To enforce these plugin standards, they maintain a blacklist of offending plugins that explains why and provides alternatives that you should use in place of them. You can search for the approved plugins and modules by visiting
`http://gulpjs.com/plugins`.

It is important to note that if you search for Gulp plugins in the npm registry, you will be shown all the plugins, including the blacklisted ones. So, just to be safe, stick to the official plugin search results to weed out any plugins that might lead you down a wrong path.
Additionally, you can run Gulp with the `--verify` flag to make it check whether any of your currently installed plugins and modules are blacklisted.

In the following tasks, I will provide you with instructions on how to install Gulp plugins as required. These will be installed in the same way we installed Gulp in Chapter 3, *Understanding the Basics of Gulp*, except now we will install multiple plugins at once. The command will look something like this:

```
npm install --save-dev gulp-plugin1 gulp-plugin2 gulp-plugin3
```

Remember, this is simply a shorthand to save you time. You could just as easily run each of these commands separately, but it would be far more verbose and unnecessary:

```
npm install --save-dev gulp-plugin1
npm install --save-dev gulp-plugin2
npm install --save-dev gulp-plugin3
```

The styles task

The first task we are going to add to our `gulpfile` will be our styles task. Our goal with this task is to combine all of our CSS files into a single file and then run those styles through a preprocessor such as Sass, Less, or Myth. In this example, we will use Myth, but you can simply substitute any other preprocessor that you would prefer to use.

Installing Gulp plugins

For this task, we will be using two plugins: `gulp-concat` and `gulp-myth`. As mentioned in the preceding section, we will install both of these tasks at the same time using the shortcut syntax. In addition to these plugins, we need to install Gulp as well, since this is the first task that we will be writing. For the remaining tasks, it won't be necessary to install Gulp again, as it will already be installed locally in our project.

Now, we need to decide which version of Gulp that we plan on using. It's suggested to go ahead and bite the bullet on version 4.x, as you will be able to take advantage of the `.series()` and `.parallel()` methods mentioned throughout the book, among other improvements.

In any case, here are the commands will need to run to install your choice of Gulp and the plugins mentioned in the previous section:

Installing Gulp 3.x:

```
npm install --save-dev gulp gulp-concat gulp-myth
```

Installing Gulp 4.x:

```
npm install --save-dev gulpjs/gulp#4.0 gulp-concat gulp-myth
```

 Once version 4.x has been officially released, you will no longer have to worry about installation using the GitHub tag, as it will take the place of the original 3.x command.

The following screenshot shows the usage of one of the commands mentioned in the preceding section:

While running these commands, make sure that you're in the root directory of your project. If you're following the naming conventions used throughout this book, then the folder should be named `gulp-book`.

Including Gulp plugins

Once complete, you will need to include references to those plugins at the beginning of your gulpfile. To do this, simply open `gulpfile.js` and add the following lines to it:

```
var gulp = require('gulp');
var concat = require('gulp-concat');
var myth = require('gulp-myth');
```

 The `gulp-myth` package is going to be used to preprocess the CSS variables we introduced in the previous chapter. This tool allows us to leverage newer CSS features in our code without being held back by browser support and adoption.

You can now match your `gulpfile` with the following screenshot:

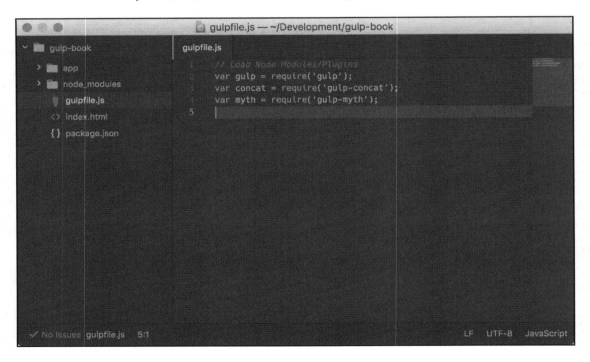

Writing the styles task

With these references added, we can now begin writing our styles task. We will start by scaffolding out the basic task method, and we will provide it with both the name of the task and the function that will execute the task's code. This initial code for the styles task is as follows:

```
gulp.task('styles', function() {
    // Code Goes Here
});
```

Next, you will need to tell Gulp where it can find the source files that you wish to process. You instruct Gulp by including a path to the file, but the path can contain globbing wildcards, such as * to reference multiple files within a single directory. To demonstrate this, we will target all of the files that are inside the css directory in our project. Take a look at the following code snippet:

```
gulp.task('styles', function() {
    return gulp.src('app/css/*.css')
        // Pipes Coming Soon
});
```

We used the * globbing pattern to tell Gulp that our source is every file with a .css extension inside of our css folder. This is a very valuable pattern that you will use constantly when writing Gulp tasks. Once our source has been set up, we can begin piping in our plugins to modify our data. We will begin by concatenating our source files into a single CSS file named all.css:

```
gulp.task('styles', function() {
    return gulp.src('app/css/*.css')
        .pipe(concat('all.css'))
        // More Pipes Coming Soon
});
```

In the preceding code, we added our concat reference that we included at the top of our gulpfile and passed it in a filename for the concatenated CSS file. In similar build systems, this would create a file and place it in a temporary location; however, with Gulp, we can send this newly created file to the next step in our pipechain without writing out to any temporary files. Next, we will pipe in our concatenated CSS file into our preprocessor:

```
gulp.task('styles', function() {
    return gulp.src('app/css/*.css')
        .pipe(concat('all.css'))
        .pipe(myth())
});
```

Finally, to finish the task, we must specify where we need to output our file. In our project, we will be outputting the file into a folder named `dist` that is located inside of our root project directory. To output a file, we will use Gulp's `.dest()` method that you learned about in Chapter 3, *Understanding the Basics of Gulp*. This expects only a single argument, namely the directory where you would like to output your processed file. The code for the `.dest()` method is as follows:

```
gulp.task('styles', function() {
    return gulp.src('app/css/*.css')
        .pipe(concat('all.css'))
        .pipe(myth())
        .pipe(gulp.dest('dist'));
});
```

You can now match your `gulpfile` with the following screenshot:

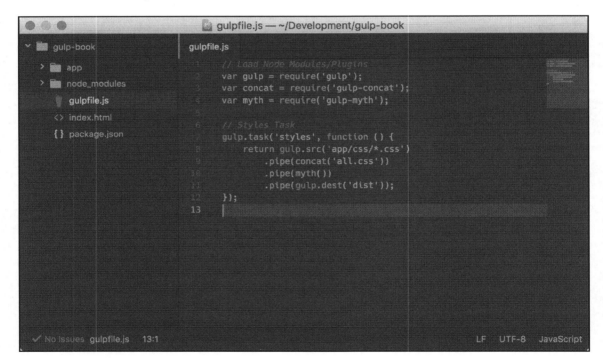

In the preceding code, we added our final pipe with the `.dest()` method and supplied it with our `dist` directory that I mentioned in one of the previous sections. This task will now put our concatenated and preprocessed file into our `dist` directory for us to include it in our application. This task is now essentially complete! We will continue to add additional functionality to it as we progress through the book, but for now our core functionality is in place.

Other preprocessors

It is important to note that concatenating our files is often not really necessary when using a preprocessor such as **Sass**. This is because it already includes an `@import` feature that allows you to separate your CSS files into partials based on their specific purpose and then pulls them all into a single file.

If you are using this functionality within Sass, then we can very easily modify our task by installing the `gulp-sass` plugin and rearranging our pipes. To do so, you would simply install the `gulp-sass` plugin and then modify your task as follows:

```
npm install gulp-sass --save-dev
```

The code for `gulp-sass` task is as follows:

```
gulp.task('styles', function() {
    return gulp.src('app/css/*.scss')
        .pipe(sass())
        .pipe(gulp.dest('dist'));
});
```

You can now remove the concatenation pipe, as the `gulp-sass` plugin will hit those imports and pull everything together for you. So, in this case, all you would need to do is simply change the source files over to `.scss` and remove the initial pipe that we used to concatenate our files. After those changes have been made, the pipechain will continue to work as expected.

Reviewing the styles task

Our styles task will first take in our CSS source files and then concatenate them into a single file that we have called `all.css`. Once they have been concatenated, we are going to pass our new `all.css` file into our pipe that will then preprocess it using `Myth` (again, you can substitute any preprocessor you prefer to use). Finally, we will save that concatenated and preprocessed file in our `dist` directory where we can finally include it in our website or application.

The scripts task

The second task will be to handle all of the JavaScript files in the project. The goal with this task is to concatenate the code into a single file, minify that code into a smaller file size, and check the code for any errors that may prevent it from running properly.

Installing Gulp plugins

For this task, we will use three plugins: `gulp-concat`, `gulp-uglify`, and `gulp -jshint`, to accomplish our goals. Like before, we will install these tasks using the shorthand syntax to save time. Since we previously installed `gulp` and `gulp-concat` while we were writing the styles task, it is unnecessary to install them again.

Instead, we will only install any new plugins and ensure they are saved to our list of development dependencies, like so:

```
npm install --save-dev gulp-uglify gulp-jshint jshint
```

You may have noticed that we're installing the `jshint` module alongside the `gulp-jshint` plugin. While we wont, be directly referencing this inside of our `gulpfile`, it is important to note that it is a required dependency of `gulp-jshint` and must be installed alongside it to work properly.

You also can match the command to the following screenshot:

```
✓ ~/Development/gulp-book
20:02 $ npm install --save-dev gulp-uglify gulp-jshint jshint
```

 When running these commands, make sure that you're in the root directory of your project. If you're following the naming conventions used throughout this book, then the folder should be named gulp-book.

Including Gulp plugins

At the top of our gulpfile, we need to add in the new Gulp plugins that we installed for this task. Once added, the top of your gulpfile should look like this:

```
var gulp = require('gulp');
var concat = require('gulp-concat');
var myth = require('gulp-myth');
var uglify = require('gulp-uglify'); // Newly Added
var jshint = require('gulp-jshint'); // Newly Added
```

The `gulpfile.js` file will now look as follows:

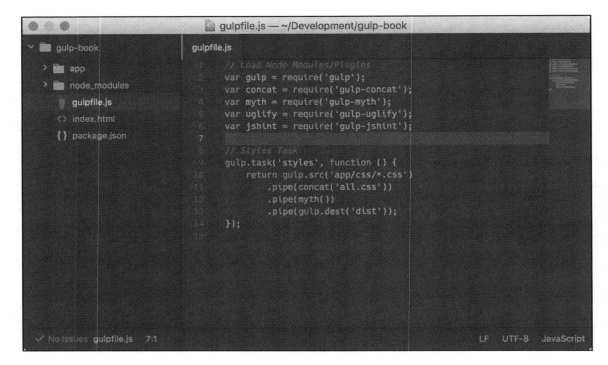

Writing the scripts task

Once the references to the new Gulp plugins have been added, we can begin writing the scripts task. Like with the styles task, we will begin by writing out the basic task structure; only this time we will provide it with the string `'scripts'` as the name for the task:

```
gulp.task('scripts', function() {
    // Code Goes Here
});
```

Like before, we will need to tell Gulp where the JavaScript source files are located using the `.src()` method. We will be using the same `*` globbing pattern that we used before to target all of the JavaScript source files in our project directory:

```
gulp.task('scripts', function() {
    return gulp.src('app/js/*.js')
        // Pipes Coming Soon
});
```

Next, we can begin adding in the pipes and plugins that we will be using in this task, the first of which will be `gulp-jshint`.

JSHint is a tool that is used to analyze JavaScript files and report any errors that could potentially break an application. The JSHint plugins also require an additional pipe that will be used to determine how errors will be reported. For this example, we are going to use the default reporter. If any errors are found, they will be output into the command-line application from where Gulp is being run:

```
gulp.task('scripts', function() {
        return gulp.src('app/js/*.js')
            .pipe(jshint())
            .pipe(jshint.reporter('default'))
            // More Pipes Coming Soon
});
```

For the next pipe, we will use `gulp-concat`. As you might recall, this is the same plugin we started with while building the styles task. As with CSS, we will concatenate all of the JavaScript files into a single file to reduce the number of requests that are needed to load our website:

```
gulp.task('scripts', function() {
        return gulp.src('app/js/*.js')
            .pipe(jshint())
            .pipe(jshint.reporter('default'))
            .pipe(concat('all.js'))
            // More Pipes Coming Soon
});
```

The next plugin we will use is `gulp-uglify`, which will minify the code to reduce the file size of the concatenated JavaScript file. This is also an important and valuable optimization:

```
gulp.task('scripts', function() {
    return gulp.src('app/js/*.js')
        .pipe(jshint())
        .pipe(jshint.reporter('default'))
        .pipe(concat('all.js'))
        .pipe(uglify())
        // Another Pipe Coming Soon
});
```

Finally, like the styles task, the final pipe will use Gulp's built-in `.dest()` method to place the processed file in the project's `dist` directory:

```
gulp.task('scripts', function() {
    return gulp.src('app/js/*.js')
        .pipe(jshint())
```

```
                    .pipe(jshint.reporter('default'))
                    .pipe(concat('all.js'))
                    .pipe(uglify())
                    .pipe(gulp.dest('dist'));
        });
```

The following screenshot is what your `gulpfile.js` should look like after the scripts task has been added:

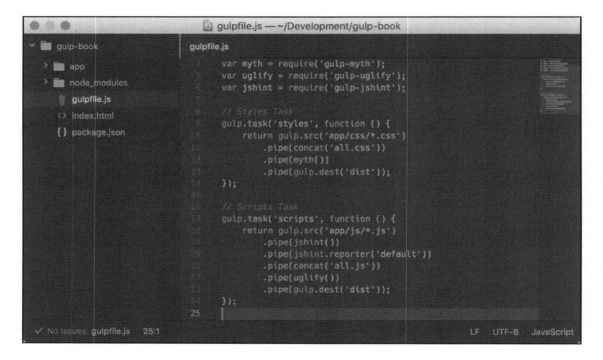

Reviewing the scripts task

The scripts task will take in all of the JavaScript files in the `app/js/` directory and then check each file for errors using the JSHint plugin. If any errors are found, they would be displayed in the command-line application using the default JSHint reporter.

Next, our JavaScript files will be concatenated into a single `all.js` file and handed off to the minification plugin, `UglifyJS`, to reduce the overall size of the file. Finally, we will output the concatenated and minified file to the project's `dist` directory.

After wrapping up the second task, you should now be able to recognize the patterns that we discussed in Chapter 3, *Understanding the Basics of Gulp*. Understanding these patterns and structures is really the most important part of learning Gulp, as everything else you will continue to learn simply builds on top of them.

The images task

The third task will handle all of the image processing. This task will be a bit smaller than the first two as it will only use a single plugin. The goal for this task is to optimize our images by minifying them, which will help reduce our payload and improve load times for our users.

Installing Gulp plugins

To minify our images, we will only use one plugin: gulp-imagemin. Like each task before it, you will need to install this locally and save it to your development dependencies as follows:

```
npm install gulp-imagemin --save-dev
```

The following two screenshots show the installation of the imagemin plugin:

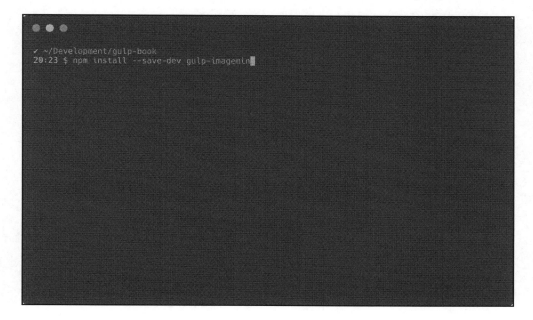

When running these commands, make sure that you're in the root directory of your project. If you're following the naming conventions used throughout this book, then the folder should be named `gulp-book`. Additionally, you may need to precede this command with sudo if you are running into permission errors.

Including Gulp plugins

With the new plugin installed, we can now add it to the top of the `gulpfile` along with the other code:

```
var gulp = require('gulp');
var concat = require('gulp-concat');
var myth = require('gulp-myth');
var uglify = require('gulp-uglify');
var jshint = require('gulp-jshint');
var imagemin = require('gulp-imagemin'); // Newly Added
```

Take a look at the following screenshot:

```
gulpfile.js — ~/Development/gulp-book

gulp-book              gulpfile.js
  app
  node_modules              // Load Node Modules/Plugins
  gulpfile.js               var gulp = require('gulp');
  <> index.html             var concat = require('gulp-concat');
  {} package.json           var myth = require('gulp-myth');
                            var uglify = require('gulp-uglify');
                            var jshint = require('gulp-jshint');
                            var imagemin = require('gulp-imagemin');
                        8   |
                            // Styles Task
                            gulp.task('styles', function () {
                                return gulp.src('app/css/*.css')
                                    .pipe(concat('all.css'))
                                    .pipe(myth())
                                    .pipe(gulp.dest('dist'));
                            });

                            // Scripts Task
                            gulp.task('scripts', function () {
                                return gulp.src('app/js/*.js')
                                    .pipe(jshint())
                                    .pipe(jshint.reporter('default'))
                                    .pipe(concat('all.js'))
  No issues gulpfile.js   8:1                          LF   UTF-8   JavaScript
```

Writing the images task

As you're probably now used to, we will start off the images task by creating a basic task definition and then using Gulp's .src() method to target all of the images in the project:

```
gulp.task('images', function() {
    return gulp.src('app/img/*')
        // Pipes Coming Soon
});
```

The only difference here is that we have not specified a filename; we are including every file that resides in the img folder. The reason for this is that throughout the course of development, it is likely that the project will use more than a single image file type. We can safely assume that there will only be images in that directory, so by targeting all of the files, we are proactively bypassing potential limitations for this task.

All that is left is to pipe in the newly added plugin followed by Gulp's .dest() method, which will save the optimized images into a new img directory alongside the optimized CSS and JavaScript files from the previous tasks:

```
gulp.task('images', function() {
    return gulp.src('app/img/*')
        .pipe(imagemin())
        .pipe(gulp.dest('dist/img'));
});
```

The following screenshot shows the code for the newly added images task:

Reviewing the images task

The images task is the smallest task yet and performs only a single action on our data. It first supplies Gulp with all of the images in our project and then runs them through our imagemin plugin to minify each file and reduce their file sizes. After this is complete, the optimized files are then passed into Gulp's `.dest()` method where they are saved inside a new `img` folder inside of the project's `dist` directory.

The watch task

So far, all of the tasks that we have written are actually only capable of running once. Once they complete, their job is considered done. However, this isn't very helpful as we would end up having to go back to our command line to run them again every time we make a change to our files. This is where Gulp's `.watch` method comes into play. The watch method's job is to specifically look for changes to files and then respond by running tasks in relation to those changes. Since we will be focusing on CSS, JavaScript, and images independently, we will need to specify three separate watch methods as well. To better organize these watch methods, we will create an additional watch task that will serve as a container and an easy way to reference all of the watch method calls inside of our `gulpfile`.

Writing the watch task

Since the watch method is built into Gulp as a core feature, no new plugins are needed. So, we can move straight to actually writing the task itself. Additionally, it will not be necessary to use the `.src()` or `.dest()` methods in this task as they have already been specified in the tasks that our watch task will reference.

As always, the first step in creating a task is to write out the basic task structure and provide it with a name. This task will be named `watch`, which is shown in the following code:

```
gulp.task('watch', function() {
    // Code Goes Here
});
```

If you can recall from `Chapter 3`, *Understanding the Basics of Gulp*, the `.watch()` method accepts two arguments. The first is a path to the file(s) that we want to monitor for changes, and the second is the name of the task that you wish to run when those files are changed.

To watch and run a single task upon a file change, you will use the following syntax:

```
gulp.task('watch', function() {
        gulp.watch('app/css/*.css', 'styles');
        gulp.watch('app/js/*.js', 'scripts');
        gulp.watch('app/img/*', 'images');
});
```

For this example project, this is all that is necessary. However, if your project requires you to run multiple tasks upon a change, you would use one of the following syntaxes depending on which version of Gulp you are using:

Using Gulp 3.x:

```
gulp.watch('app/css/*.css', ['firstTask', 'secondTask']);
gulp.watch('app/js/*.js', ['thirdTask', 'fourthTask']);
```

Using Gulp 4.x:

```
gulp.watch('app/css/*.css', gulp.parallel('firstTask', 'secondTask'));
gulp.watch('app/js/*.js', gulp.series('thirdTask', 'fourthTask'));
```

The main difference between these two examples is that for version 3.x all tasks must be ran concurrently, while version 4.x provides us with the `.series()` and `.parallel()` methods, so we can have more explicit control of the execution order of our tasks.

The method that you use will depend on your project. If any of your tasks require another task to finish completely before moving to the next, then you should use the .series() method. The .series() method will ensure that all tasks execute in the order that they are listed. Alternatively, the .parallel() method acts much like the 3.x example in that it will run all listed tasks concurrently. Take a look at the following screenshot:

In the preceding code, we created three .watch() methods: one for our CSS, one for our JavaScript, and one for our images. In each of these, we provide the method with the path to those files and follow that up with the name of the task we want to run if those files are modified. When this task is run, Gulp will continuously look for changes to the files located in those paths, and if any of those files change, Gulp will run the task that is specified in the second argument. This will continue to happen until Gulp is manually stopped.

Reviewing the watch task

The watch task is one of the most unique tasks that we have written, simply because it is more of a *helper task* that provides helpful functionality. It's not using or running any build-specific actions; it is only giving us more control over when our tasks can be run and allowing us to automate the execution of tasks.

The default task

Our final task is the default task, and it is best considered as the entry point for our `gulpfile`. The purpose of this task is to gather and execute any tasks that Gulp needs to run by default.

Writing the default task

The default task is the smallest and the most simple task in our `gulpfile` and will only take up a single line of code. For this task, we only need to provide it with the name default and the tasks we would like to run by default.

Using Gulp 3.x:

```
gulp.task('default', ['styles', 'scripts', 'images', 'watch']);
```

Using Gulp 4.x:

```
gulp.task('default', gulp.parallel('styles', 'scripts', 'images', 'watch'));
```

After adding the default task, our `gulpfile` should look like this:

This code will run each of our tasks once, including our watch task. The watch task will continuously check for changes to our files after the initial round of processing is complete and re-run each of our tasks when the related files change.

Completed gulpfile

Congratulations! You have written your very first `gulpfile`. However, this is only scratching the surface. We have a lot more to add in the coming chapters, including using Node.js modules for advanced tasks, as well as some great tips and improvements. Before we move on, let's take a moment to review the completed file that we created in this chapter. This is a great opportunity to compare your file with the code given and ensure that your code matches with what we have written so far. This may save your debugging time later!

The completed `gulpfile` should look as follows:

```
// Modules & Plugins
var gulp = require('gulp');
var concat = require('gulp-concat');
var myth = require('gulp-myth');
var uglify = require('gulp-uglify');
var jshint = require('gulp-jshint');
var imagemin = require('gulp-imagemin');

// Styles Task
gulp.task('styles', function () {
    return gulp.src('app/css/*.css')
        .pipe(concat('all.css'))
        .pipe(myth())
        .pipe(gulp.dest('dist'));
});

// Scripts Task
gulp.task('scripts', function () {
    return gulp.src('app/js/*.js')
        .pipe(jshint())
        .pipe(jshint.reporter('default'))
        .pipe(concat('all.js'))
        .pipe(uglify())
        .pipe(gulp.dest('dist'));
});

// Images Task
gulp.task('images', function () {
    return gulp.src('app/img/*')
```

```
        .pipe(imagemin())
        .pipe(gulp.dest('dist/img'));
});

// Watch Task
gulp.task('watch', function () {
    gulp.watch('app/css/*.css', 'styles');
    gulp.watch('app/js/*.js', 'scripts');
    gulp.watch('app/img/*', 'images');
});

// Default Task
gulp.task('default', ['styles', 'scripts', 'images', 'watch']);
```

Running tasks

Now that our `gulpfile` is complete, it is time to learn how to run each of the tasks that we have written. In this section, you will learn more about our default task and how to target and run any of our tasks independently.

Running the default task

In many cases, gulpfiles are structured to be executed with a single one, word command, `gulp`. Upon running this command, Gulp will run the task with the name default in our `gulpfile`. As you may recall from the previous section, that is why it is considered to be the entry point. When running Gulp like this, without any additional parameters, it is built to always run the default task, which in turn can run any number of tasks that we created.

Running a single task

Some projects may require that a task be run independently and manually as a certain step in the workflow process. If you need to run any of the tasks manually, you can do so by simply separating your Gulp command with a single space and then listing the name of the task that you wish to run as a parameter. For example, the following command will only run our styles task:

gulp styles

You can do this with any of the tasks that you have included in your `gulpfile`, even your watch or default tasks. The important thing to remember is that if you don't specify a task, then Gulp will automatically choose to run the default task for you.

So, consider that you run the following command:

```
gulp default
```

This is essentially the same as running the following:

```
gulp
```

Stopping a watch task

Tasks are designed to run through their process and once they are completed, Gulp will exit and return you to your Command Prompt. However, running a task that uses the `.watch()` method instructs Gulp to continue listening for changes to your files beyond the initial execution. So, once a task is executed that uses a `.watch()` method, Gulp will not stop unless it runs into an error or until you specifically instruct it to stop.

For beginners, this can be quite confusing, especially if you are still getting accustomed to the command line. The important thing to remember is that you must always manually stop an operation in progress using the *Ctrl + C* key combination. This will end the process and return you to your command prompt to run more commands.

Summary

In this chapter, you learned how to write and run a fully functional `gulpfile` from the ground up. In it, we created three tasks to process our CSS, JavaScript, and image files.

Our CSS task joins together all of our CSS files and then passes the joined file through a preprocessor so that we can use cutting-edge CSS features such as variables and mathematical calculations.

Our JavaScript task uses a linter to analyze our code for any errors, concatenate those files, and minify the combined file to reduce its overall file size.

Lastly, we created tasks to optimize our image files, watch our source files for changes, and determine which tasks are run by default.

In the next chapter, we will take a look at how to use Node.js modules in place of Gulp plugins to add advanced functionality to your projects.

5

Creating Advanced Tasks

Until now, we have only explored basic implementations of Gulp plugins to handle the various tasks that we've built in our `gulpfile`. In this chapter, you are going to learn how to use plain Node.js modules in our Gulp tasks and explore new ways to create tasks using plugins and node modules together.

Using plain Node.js modules

Using Gulp plugins is the easiest way to add functionality to your workflow. However, the actions that you need to perform inside your tasks are sometimes better off being written using plain Node.js modules and occasionally you will need to use plugins and Node.js modules together.

In this section, we will cover common usage of plain Node.js modules, when and why these modules should be used in place of (or alongside of) Gulp plugins, and some various examples you can use in your own gulpfile to improve your builds.

Why use plain Node.js modules?

A common misunderstanding and topic of confusion for Gulp beginners is when and why to use plain Node.js modules in place of using or creating a new Gulp plugin. Generally, the best practice is that if you *can* use plain Node.js modules, then you *should* use plain Node.js modules.

Gulp was built on the Unix philosophy that we can pull together many smaller, single-purpose applications to perform more complex actions. With this philosophy we are never duplicating work or introducing redundant plugins into the community. Additionally, it is easier to test the expectations of each smaller application than it would be to test a large collection of duplicated code.

The Gulp team spends a lot of time ensuring that their plugin ecosystem remains healthy and uncluttered with redundancy. Part of ensuring this is making sure that no Gulp plugin deviates from this core philosophy. Any Gulp plugin that doesn't follow it are added to a community-driven blacklist and will not be displayed to other users in the official Gulp plugin search. This is very important to remember when looking for plugins to use, or if you ever plan on creating a plugin yourself. Don't duplicate work that has already been done. If you would like to help improve a plugin, contact the maintainer and work together to improve it for everyone so we can all keep the plugin ecosystem lean and focused.

If we all decided to create our own version of every plugin, then the ecosystem would be inundated with duplication, which would only confuse users and damage the overall perception of Gulp as a tool.

 If you're ever unsure if the plugins you are using have been blacklisted, you can run the `gulp --verify` command to check if they are included on the official Gulp blacklist.

Static server

For quick and easy distribution, having the ability to spin up a small file server can be a great time saver and will prevent the need to run larger server software such as Apache or Nginx.

For this task, instead of using a Gulp plugin, we are going to use the **Connect middleware framework** module. Middleware is a small layer that allows us to build additional functionality into our applications, or in this case, our Gulp tasks.

Connect itself only acts as the framework to pull in additional functionality, so in addition to Connect, we will need to install the plugin that we wish to use. To spin up a static server, we will be using the `serve-static` Node.js module.

Installing modules

Installing plain Node.js modules is exactly the same process as installing Gulp plugins because, despite the Gulp focus, Gulp plugins are still Node.js modules at heart. The modules we will be using for this specific task are `connect` and `serve-static`.

To install `connect` and `serve-static`, we will run the following command:

```
npm install connect serve-static --save-dev
```

The following screenshot reflects the command to install the modules that we will use to create our server task:

Including modules

As you might expect, we will include any plain Node.js modules in the same way that we included our Gulp plugins from the previous chapter. We will be adding these two to the bottom of our code as shown in the following code snippet:

```
// Load Node Modules/Plugins
var gulp = require('gulp');
var concat = require('gulp-concat');
var myth = require('gulp-myth');
var uglify = require('gulp-uglify');
var jshint = require('gulp-jshint');
var imagemin = require('gulp-imagemin');
var connect = require('connect'); // Added
var serve = require('serve-static'); // Added
```

The updated `gulpfile` should look like this:

```
gulpfile.js — ~/Development/gulp-book
gulpfile.js
     // Load Node Modules/Plugins
     var gulp = require('gulp');
     var concat = require('gulp-concat');
     var myth = require('gulp-myth');
     var uglify = require('gulp-uglify');
     var jshint = require('gulp-jshint');
     var imagemin = require('gulp-imagemin');
     var connect = require('connect');
   9 var serve = require('serve-static');

     // Styles Task
     gulp.task('styles', function () {
        return gulp.src('app/css/*.css')
            .pipe(concat('all.css'))
            .pipe(myth())
            .pipe(gulp.dest('dist'));
     });

     // Scripts Task
     gulp.task('scripts', function () {
```

`No Issues   gulpfile.js   9:37                                    LF   UTF-8   JavaScript`

Writing server task

Once our Node.js modules have been installed and included, we can begin writing our new task. We will introduce some more advanced Node.js-specific syntax, but it will most likely feel somewhat familiar to the tasks we created in the previous chapter.

Our server task will look like this:

```
// Server Task
gulp.task('server', function() {
  return connect().use(serve(__dirname))
    .listen(8080)
    .on('listening', function() {
      console.log('Server Running: View at http://localhost:8080');
    });
});
```

The following screenshot shows the newly added server task in our gulpfile:

```
● ● ●                    ≡ gulpfile.js — ~/Development/gulp-book
 gulpfile.js
 31        return gulp.src('app/img/*')
 32            .pipe(imagemin())
 33            .pipe(gulp.dest('dist/img'));
 34    });
 35
 36    // Server Task
 37    gulp.task('server', function() {
 38        return connect().use(serve(__dirname))
 39            .listen(8080)
 40            .on('listening', function() {
 41                console.log('Server Running: View at http://localhost:8080');
 42            });
 43    });
 44
 45    // Watch Task
 46    gulp.task('watch', function () {
 47        gulp.watch('app/css/*.css', ['styles', browsersync.reload]);
 48        gulp.watch('app/js/*.js', ['scripts', browsersync.reload]);
 49        gulp.watch('app/img/*', ['images', browsersync.reload]);
 50    });
 ✓ No Issues  gulpfile.js   43:4                                    LF   UTF-8   JavaScript
```

The first thing you will notice is that aside from our main .task() wrapper method, we don't actually use Gulp at all in this task. It's literally a wrapper to label and run the Node.js code that resides within.

Let's take a moment to discuss this code to better understand what it does—we include our connect() function. Next, we will use its .use() method and pass it to our serve() module. In the serve() module, we will pass it to the directory we wish to serve from; in our case __dirname, which is used by Node.js to output the name of the directory that the currently executing script resides in. Next, we assign port 8080 to listen for requests. Finally, we use the .on() method to check whether our server is successfully listening, and then we log a small command to announce that the server is running as expected.

Compared to the Gulp tasks we've created thus far, not a lot has changed. The only difference is that we are using the methods for the plain Node.js module instead of Gulp's built-in methods such as `.src()` and `.dest()`. That's because in this case we aren't actually using Gulp to modify any data. We are only using it to label, organize, and control the use of a plain Node.js module within a Gulp task. The server doesn't have any use for modifying our data or using streams; it simply exists as a way to serve the files to a browser.

Finally, if you would like, you can include this task inside your default task so that this task is run by default.

When added, your default task should now look like the following:

Using Gulp 3.x:

```
// Default Task
gulp.task('default', ['styles', 'scripts', 'images', 'server',
'watch']);
```

Using Gulp 4.x:

```
// Default Task
gulp.task('default', gulp.parallel('styles', 'scripts', 'images',
'server', 'watch'));
```

BrowserSync

As web developers, we spend a lot of time interacting with our browsers. Whether we are debugging our code, resizing our windows, or simply refreshing our pages, we often perform a lot of repetitive tasks in order to do our jobs.

In this section, we will explore ways to eliminate browser refreshes and make some other handy improvements to our browser experience. To do this, we will use an incredible Node.js module called **BrowserSync**.

BrowserSync is one of the most impressive tools I have ever used. Upon first use, it will truly wow you with what it is capable of doing. Unlike similar tools that only handle browser refreshing, BrowserSync will additionally sync up every action that is performed on your pages across any device on your local network.

This process allows you to have multiple devices viewing the same project simultaneously and maintains actions, such as scrolling, in sync across them all. It's really quite impressive and can save you a ton of time when developing, especially if you're working on responsive designs.

Installing BrowserSync

To use BrowserSync, we first need to install it. The process is the same as all of the other plugins and modules that we have installed previously.

To install BrowserSync, run the following command:

```
npm install --save-dev browser-sync
```

As always, we will include our `--save-dev` flag to ensure that it is added to our development dependencies list. Take a look at the following screenshot:

Including BrowserSync

Once installed, we can add the module to our project by adding it to our list of requires at the top of our `gulpfile`.

The module/plugin to be included in the code is as follows:

```
// Load Node Modules/Plugins
var gulp = require('gulp');
var concat = require('gulp-concat');
var myth = require('gulp-myth');
var uglify = require('gulp-uglify');
var jshint = require('gulp-jshint');
var imagemin = require('gulp-imagemin');
var connect = require('connect');
var serve = require('server-static');
var browsersync = require('browser-sync'); // Added
```

The following screenshot shows the newly required `browsersync` module in our `gulpfile`:

Writing the BrowserSync task

Now, let's create a small task that we can call anytime we need to communicate any changes we make to our browsers as shown in the following code snippet:

```
// BrowserSync Task
gulp.task('browsersync', function() {
    return browsersync({
        server: {
            baseDir: './'
        }
    });
});
```

The following screenshot shows the completed BrowserSync task in our `gulpfile`:

In this task, we have simply called our `browsersync` module and provided it with our base project directory as the location to create the server instance.

As a final step, we need to add some additional information to our watch task to let BrowserSync know when to reload our browsers:

Use the following code for version 4.x:

```
// Watch Task
 gulp.task('watch', function() {
    gulp.watch('app/css/*.css', gulp.series('styles',
browsersync.reload));
    gulp.watch('app/js/*.js', gulp.series('scripts',
browsersync.reload));
    gulp.watch('app/img/*', gulp.series('images', browsersync.reload));
});
```

Use the following code for version 3.x:

```
// Watch Task
gulp.task('watch', function() {
    gulp.watch('app/css/*.css', ['styles', browsersync.reload]);
    gulp.watch('app/js/*.js', ['scripts', browsersync.reload]);
    gulp.watch('app/img/*', ['images', browsersync.reload]);
});
```

Now, we need our watch methods to run two items instead of one. So, in the version 4.x example we have added in the .series() method to execute our tasks in a specified order. In the series method, we will pass in our task name first, and then include a reference to the .reload() method of our browsersync task. This will allow our tasks to complete before communicating any changes to our source files and instruct BrowserSync to refresh our browsers.

If you would like this task to run by default, be sure that you also include it to your default task as follows:

Use the following code for Gulp 4.x:

```
// Default Task
 gulp.task('default', gulp.parallel('styles', 'scripts', 'images',
'browsersync', 'watch'));
```

Use the following code for Gulp 3.x:

```
// Default Task
 gulp.task('default', ['styles', 'scripts', 'images', 'browsersync',
'watch']);
```

The following screenshot shows the updated default task:

```
● ● ●                    ≡ gulpfile.js — ~/Development/gulp-book

gulpfile.js

46    // BrowserSync Task
47    gulp.task('browsersync', function() {
48        return browsersync({
49            server: {
50                baseDir: './'
51            }
52        });
53    });
54
55    // Watch Task
56    gulp.task('watch', function () {
57        gulp.watch('app/css/*.css', ['styles', browsersync.reload]);
58        gulp.watch('app/js/*.js', ['scripts', browsersync.reload]);
59        gulp.watch('app/img/*', ['images', browsersync.reload]);
60    });
61
62    // Default Task
63    gulp.task('default', ['styles', 'scripts', 'images', 'browsersync', 'watch']);
64

✓ No issues  gulpfile.js    53:4                              LF    UTF-8    JavaScript
```

Going into a lot of detail about BrowserSync is really out of the scope of this book; however, it's worth knowing what to expect when you run this task. As soon as Gulp runs our `browsersync` task, it will immediately create a server and open a new browser window pointing to `http://localhost:3000`, which is the default port that BrowserSync uses. Once this has been completed, everything that runs on that page will be automatically refreshed if you update your code.

Additionally, you will be given an external URL that you can visit on other devices, such as a phone or tablet, as long as they are all on the same network. Once you have visited that URL, all of your actions will be kept in sync and any time you make changes to your code, all of the devices will refresh to show those changes automatically. It even tracks your scrolling movement on every single device, so if you decide to scroll up on your phone, the website will also scroll up on every other device, including your laptop or computer. It's an incredibly neat and helpful tool.

 It is worth noting that using *both* a static server and BrowserSync are unnecessary as they serve a similar purpose. It's really dependent on which suits your project best. In most cases, I would suggest using BrowserSync due to the added features that it provides.

PostCSS

Our plugin usage up to this point has been very basic, so we're going to take a moment to revisit our styles task to replace the Myth plugin with a more advanced tool called **PostCSS**. While Myth is very easy to set up and begin using, there are times when a project may require specific processing of CSS files. PostCSS breaks apart the processing work into individual modules that you can use separately or combine as needed.

For the purpose of this update, we're only going to worry about replicating the functionality we were using within Myth and to demonstrate how Gulp plugins and node modules can work together to create more robust tasks.

Removing Myth plugin

First, let's start by removing the gulp-myth plugin from our project:

```
npm uninstall --save-dev gulp-myth
```

The following screenshot reflects the command to install this plugin:

This will uninstall the gulp-myth plugin and remove it from our development dependencies list in our package.json file.

Next, we can remove all current references to Myth in our `gulpfile`. You can see the following code snippets to make sure your required plugins and styles task have been properly removed:

```
// Load Node Modules/Plugins
var gulp = require('gulp');
var concat = require('gulp-concat');
var uglify = require('gulp-uglify');
var jshint = require('gulp-jshint');
var imagemin = require('gulp-imagemin');
var connect = require('connect');
var serve = require('server-static');
var browsersync = require('browser-sync');
```

The required code snippet for styles is as follows:

```
// Styles Task
gulp.task('styles', function () {
    return gulp.src('app/css/*.css')
        .pipe(concat('all.css'))
        .pipe(gulp.dest('dist'));
});
```

This screenshot shows the changes to our `gulpfile` once we have removed the `gulp-myth` plugin:

Installing modules

With `Myth` now removed, we can now install the new plugins and node modules we will be using to replace it. In this example, we will be installing `gulp-postcss`, `postcss-cssnext`, and `cssnano`. The first being the `PostCSS` Gulp plugin, the second being the `CSSNext` plugin for `PostCSS`, and the third being `CSSNano`, a basic node module used to minify CSS. Refer to the following command:

```
npm install --save-dev gulp-postcss postcss-cssnext cssnano
```

The following screenshot reflects the command to install the new plugins and modules:

Including modules

With these plugins installed, we can now add them to the top of our `gulpfile` as shown in the following code snippet:

```
// Load Node Modules/Plugins
var gulp = require('gulp');
var concat = require('gulp-concat');
var uglify = require('gulp-uglify');
var jshint = require('gulp-jshint');
```

```
var imagemin = require('gulp-imagemin');
var connect = require('connect');
var serve = require('serve-static');
var browsersync = require('browser-sync');
var postcss = require('gulp-postcss'); // Added
var cssnext = require('postcss-cssnext'); // Added
var cssnano = require('cssnano'); // Added
```

The following screenshot shows the newly required modules in our `gulpfile`:

Updating the styles task

Next, let's go back to our styles task and add in our newly required PostCSS plugin in our pipechain where the `Myth` plugin used to be:

```
// Styles Task
gulp.task('styles', function () {
    return gulp.src('app/css/*.css')
        .pipe(concat('all.css'))
        .pipe(postcss())
        .pipe(gulp.dest('dist'));
});
```

This screenshot demonstrates the implementation of the `gulp-postcss` plugin in the `styles` pipechain:

```
● ● ●                    ☰ gulpfile.js — ~/Development/gulp-book
gulpfile.js
          var serve = require('serve-static');
          var browsersync = require('browser-sync');
          var postcss = require('gulp-postcss');
          var cssnext = require('postcss-cssnext');
          var cssnano = require('cssnano');

          // Styles Task
          gulp.task('styles', function () {
              return gulp.src('app/css/*.css')
                  .pipe(concat('all.css'))
    18            .pipe(postcss())
                  .pipe(gulp.dest('dist'));
          });

          // Scripts Task
          gulp.task('scripts', function () {
              return gulp.src('app/js/*.js')
                  .pipe(jshint())
                  .pipe(jshint.reporter('default'))
✓ No Issues  gulpfile.js   18:25                              LF   UTF-8   JavaScript
```

Now that we have added the plugin to the pipechain, we need to provide it with the other accompanying plugins we installed so that we can perform those specified transforms on our CSS. To do this, we will need to do something a bit different than the previous examples. We're going to pass an array as an argument PostCSS plugin. Inside of that array, we will reference the other modules we'll be using to transform our CSS. Refer to the following code snippet:

```
// Styles Task
gulp.task('styles', function () {
    return gulp.src('app/css/*.css')
        .pipe(concat('all.css'))
        .pipe(postcss([
            cssnext(),
            cssnano()
        ]))
        .pipe(gulp.dest('dist'));
});
```

The following screenshot demonstrates how we add the installed plugins as arguments to the PostCSS:

```
● ● ●                    ≡ gulpfile.js — ~/Development/gulp-book
gulpfile.js
 10    var postcss = require('gulp-postcss');
 11    var cssnext = require('postcss-cssnext');
 12    var cssnano = require('cssnano');
 13
 14    // Styles Task
 15    gulp.task('styles', function () {
 16        return gulp.src('app/css/*.css')
 17            .pipe(concat('all.css'))
 18            .pipe(postcss([
 19                cssnext(),
 20                cssnano()
 21            ]))
 22            .pipe(gulp.dest('dist'));
 23    });
 24
 25    // Scripts Task
 26    gulp.task('scripts', function () {
 27        return gulp.src('app/js/*.js')
 28            .pipe(jshint())
             .pipe(jshint.reporter('default'))
 ✓ No issues  gulpfile.js   15:34                              LF    UTF-8    JavaScript
```

Now, we have fully functioning styles task using PostCSS in place of Myth. This will give us a bit more flexibility to add in additional transforms to our CSS as our project grows.

 You may notice a warning about autoprefixer being executed multiple times when you run this task. As of today, this is due to both plugins depending on autoprefixer but using them in different ways. CSSNano is using autoprefixer to remove unnecessary browser prefixes from the CSS while PostCSS is using autoprefixer to add them. You can prevent this warning by updating your CSSNano reference like so: `cssnano({autoprefixer: false})`.

Browserify

As you have now experienced when creating a gulpfile and writing tasks, the way Node.js breaks code into modules is very clean and natural. With node.js we can assign an entire module to a variable using node.js' `require()` function.

This pattern is actually based on a specification called **CommonJS** and it is a truly fantastic way to organize and modularize code. Browserify is a tool that was created to leverage that exact same specification so that you can write all of your JavaScript code that way. Not only will you be able to modularize your own project code, but you now have the ability to use modules from npm in your non-Node.js JavaScript. It's quite remarkable.

The goal of this task is to use Browserify so that we can write our JavaScript files using the CommonJS spec that Node.js uses to include and modularize various pieces of our application. Additionally, we will also be able to use many other Node.js modules in our projects on the client side without having to run them on a server.

 It is important to note that this is an alternative to our currently created scripts task, which is why we're creating a separate task altogether. So, only one of these would be necessary in your projects. It's all depending on your project needs and how you would prefer to organize your code.

Installing modules

We will use the `browserify`, `vinyl-source-stream`, and `vinyl-buffer` modules for this task. Many node.js modules operate using Node.js streams, but Gulp uses a virtual file format called vinyl to process files. So, to interact with modules such as Browserify, we must convert the stream into a format that we can use by including the `vinyl-source-steam` module.

To install these modules, run the following command:

```
npm install --save-dev browserify vinyl-source-stream vinyl-buffer
```

The following screenshot reflects the command to install Browserify and the related node modules:

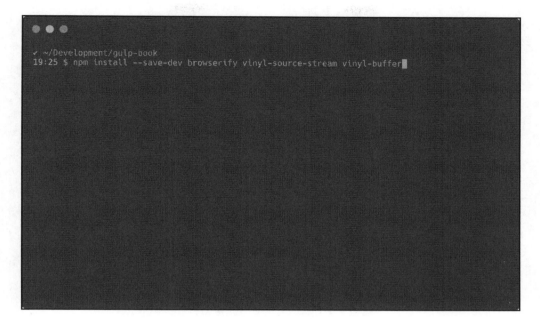

Including modules

Once we have installed our modules, we can add them to our `gulpfile` by appending them to our list of requires, like this:

```
// Load Node Modules/Plugins
var gulp = require('gulp');
var concat = require('gulp-concat');
var uglify = require('gulp-uglify');
var jshint = require('gulp-jshint');
var imagemin = require('gulp-imagemin');
var connect = require('connect');
var serve = require('server-static');
var browsersync = require('browser-sync');
var postcss = require('gulp-postcss');
var cssnext = require('postcss-cssnext');
var cssnano = require('cssnano');
var browserify = require('browserify'); // Added
var source = require('vinyl-source-stream'); // Added
var buffer = require('vinyl-buffer'); // Added
```

The following screenshot shows the newly required modules in our `gulpfile`:

Writing the Browserify task

As with all of our other tasks, we always start with our main task wrapper method and provide our task with a name. In this task, we will blend new methods from our Browserify module with some of Gulp's methods that you are already familiar with.

Let's add in the code for our new `browserify` task:

```
// Browserify Task
gulp.task('browserify', function() {
  return browserify('./app/js/app.js')
    .bundle()
    .pipe(source('bundle.js'))
    .pipe(buffer())
    .pipe(gulp.dest('dist'));
});
```

This screenshot demonstrates how to build our the new Browserify task in our `gulpfile`:

```
● ● ●                    ≡ gulpfile.js — ~/Development/gulp-book

gulpfile.js
 61        });
 62      });
 63
 64      // Browserify Task
 65      gulp.task('browserify', function() {
 66          return browserify('./app/js/app.js')
 67              .bundle()
 68              .pipe(source('bundle.js'))
 69              .pipe(buffer())
 70              .pipe(gulp.dest('dist'));
 71      });
 72
 73      // Watch Task
 74      gulp.task('watch', function () {
 75          gulp.watch('app/css/*.css', ['styles', browsersync.reload]);
 76          gulp.watch('app/js/*.js', ['scripts', browsersync.reload]);
 77          gulp.watch('app/img/*', ['images', browsersync.reload]);
 78      });
 79
 80      // Default Task
 ✓ No Issues  gulpfile.js  71:4                        LF   UTF-8   JavaScript
```

To better understand what is happening in this task, let's break it down into steps:

1. First, we pass our main JavaScript application that requires our modules to `browserify()`.

2. We then run Browserify's built-in `.bundle()` method, which will bundle our source file and its dependencies into a single file.

3. The file then gets passed to our first `.pipe()` method, which uses `vinyl-source-stream` to convert the Node.js stream into a vinyl stream, and then we provide the bundle with the name `bundle.js`.

4. Next, we turn the vinyl stream into a vinyl buffer so that we can then pass the data into other Gulp plugins such as `gulp-uglify`. This step is required because some Gulp plugins require the data to be a buffer instead of a stream before processing. We can begin piping in any of our Gulp plugins after this pipe and before the next pipe.

5. Once our file has been bundled, processed, and named, we finally pass it to our final pipe, which uses the `.dest()` method to output the file.

The only really confusing portion of this task is understanding the difference between Node.js streams and Gulp streams. Beyond that, the task runs somewhat like our original Gulp tasks, which we created in the previous chapter. Knowing when and how to work around the differences in streams will make your life a lot easier when using plain Node.js modules inside of Gulp tasks.

 As with all tasks, if you would like this to be run by default or have it run upon file changes, be sure that you also include it in your default and/or watch tasks as we have done throughout the book.

While this task sets you up to use Browserify inside Gulp, you should take some time to really understand how Browserify works and how to make use of it in your projects. To learn more about Browserify, be sure to check out the official site at `http://browserify.org`.

Babel

Now that we have our Browserify build setup, we can introduce additional plugins to the build that will give us more ways to enhance our code. In this section, we're going to add Babel, and more specifically the `babelify` module, to our Browserify task.

Babel is another popular tool that enables us to use cutting edge JavaScript features in our code without having to wait on browser vendors to implement the functionality. Babel does this by passing our code through various presets that handle specific feature implementations such as ES2015, ES2016, and beyond.

The beauty behind this is that as those features are introduced in browsers natively, we can easily remove the presets that are no longer needed and our build will continue to work.

 For more information on Babel and how to take advantage of the latest features of JavaScript, visit the official Babel website: `https://babeljs.io /learn-es2015/`

Installing modules

To implement this, we'll need to install some new modules such as `babelify` and a preset that will allow us to use the latest JavaScript features:

```
npm install --save-dev babelify babel-preset-env
```

The following screenshot reflects the command to install `babelify` and the related `babel` plugin:

Including modules

Next, we will need to require the `babelify` module at the top of our `gulpfile`:

```
// Load Node Modules/Plugins
var gulp = require('gulp');
var concat = require('gulp-concat');
var uglify = require('gulp-uglify');
var jshint = require('gulp-jshint');
var imagemin = require('gulp-imagemin');
var connect = require('connect');
var serve = require('server-static');
var postcss = require('gulp-postcss');
var cssnext = require('postcss-cssnext');
var cssnano = require('cssnano');
var browsersync = require('browser-sync');
var browserify = require('browserify');
var source = require('vinyl-source-stream');
var buffer = require('vinyl-buffer');
var babelify = require('babelify'); // Added
```

The following screenshot shows the newly required `babelify` module in our `gulpfile`:

```
gulpfile.js — ~/Development/gulp-book
gulpfile.js
1   // Load Node Modules/Plugins
2   var gulp = require('gulp');
3   var concat = require('gulp-concat');
4   var uglify = require('gulp-uglify');
5   var jshint = require('gulp-jshint');
6   var imagemin = require('gulp-imagemin');
7   var connect = require('connect');
8   var serve = require('serve-static');
9   var browsersync = require('browser-sync');
10  var postcss = require('gulp-postcss');
11  var cssnext = require('postcss-cssnext');
12  var cssnano = require('cssnano');
13  var browserify = require('browserify');
14  var source = require('vinyl-source-stream');
15  var buffer = require('vinyl-buffer');
16  var babelify = require('babelify');
17
18  // Styles Task
19  gulp.task('styles', function () {
```

Update Browserify task

With these modules installed and `babelify` required, we can now update our `browserify` task by adding in a new transform and providing the transform with the presets that we wish to use on our JavaScript. In this case, we will be using the `env` preset as shown in the following code snippet:

```
gulp.task('browserify', function() {
    return browserify('./app/js/app.js')
        .transform('babelify', {
            presets: ['env']
        })
        .bundle()
        .pipe(source('bundle.js'))
        .pip(buffer())
        .pipe(gulp.dest('dist'));
});
```

The following screenshot demonstrates how we can add the `babelify` transform to our `browserify` task:

```
● ● ●                    ≡ gulpfile.js — ~/Development/gulp-book
gulpfile.js
  61        });
  62    });
  63
  64    // Browserify Task
  65    gulp.task('browserify', function() {
  66        return browserify('./app/js/app.js')
  67            .transform('babelify', {
  68                presets: ['env']
  69            })
  70            .bundle()
  71            .pipe(source('bundle.js'))
  72            .pipe(buffer())
  73            .pipe(gulp.dest('dist'));
  74    });
  75
  76    // Watch Task
  77    gulp.task('watch', function () {
  78        gulp.watch('app/css/*.css', ['styles', browsersync.reload]);
  79        gulp.watch('app/js/*.js', ['scripts', browsersync.reload]);
                gulp.watch('app/img/*' ['images' browsersync reload]);
✓ No Issues  gulpfile.js    69:11                                      LF    UTF-8    JavaScript
```

Summary

In this chapter, we took a look at three advanced tasks using plain Node.js modules instead of Gulp plugins. Our first task creates a simple static server so that we can view our project in a browser. The second assists us by automatically refreshing our browser and keeping our actions in sync across multiple devices as we work. The third task allows us to use the Node.js/CommonJS spec to modularize our client-side code and write it as if it is a Node.js application. Finally, we implemented Babel as a part of our Browserify task so that we can use the latest JavaScript features in our code without worrying about browser implementation.

In the next chapter, we will continue to improve our `gulpfile` by taking a look at some valuable tips and resolve some common issues that are easy to run into while using Gulp.

6
Tips, Tricks, and Resolving Issues

By this point, we have highlighted the many ways through which Gulp will improve your workflow and help you deliver more optimized and performant code. As with all software, there are some quirks that you may run into while using Gulp that could make the experience less than perfect.

In this chapter, we will explore some common tips, tricks, and solutions to some of the troubles that you may run into while using Gulp.

Handling errors

One of the biggest problems that I encountered when first learning Gulp was how to handle it when something failed. Unfortunately, gulp doesn't have a clean way to handle errors, and when failures do occur, it doesn't handle them very gracefully. For example, let's say we have our watch task running in the background as we are editing a Sass file. We're typing away and styling our website, but we accidentally hit a key that the `Sass` plugin wasn't expecting. Instead of failing through the code and just displaying the page break at that moment, Gulp will simply throw an error and the watch task will stop running.

The main problem with this is that you may not actually realize that Gulp has stopped and you will continue working on your code, only to realize moments later that all of your changes aren't being reflected on the page you are working on. It can cause a lot of confusion and end up wasting a lot of time until you know when to expect it.

The Gulp team acknowledge that this is one of the pain points when using Gulp and they realize the importance of improving it. Fortunately, they are considering this issue as one of the highest priorities for future development. There are plans to include improved error handling in the upcoming versions of Gulp. However, until then we can still improve our error handling by introducing a new Gulp plugin called `gulp-plumber`.

The `gulp-plumber` plugin was created as a stop-gap to give us more control over handling errors in our tasks. Let's take a look at how we can include it in our styles task that we created in `Chapter 3`, *Performing Tasks with Gulp*.

Installing gulp-plumber

Before we can begin using the plugin, we need to install it and save it to our development dependencies.

The command for installing `gulp-plumber` is as follows:

```
npm install --save-dev gulp-plumber
```

The following screenshot reflects the command we will run to install the Gulp plugin:

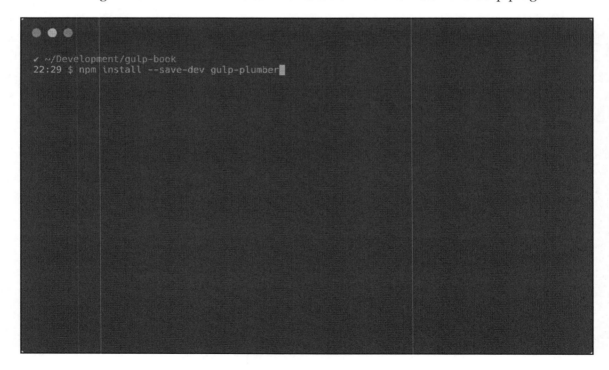

Including gulp-plumber

After installation, we must add it to our list of requirements to include it in our `gulpfile`:

```
// Load Node Modules/Plugins
var gulp = require('gulp');
var concat = require('gulp-concat');
var uglify = require('gulp-uglify');
var jshint = require('gulp-jshint');
var imagemin = require('gulp-imagemin');
var connect = require('connect');
var serve = require('serve-static');
var browsersync = require('browser-sync');
var postcss = require('gulp-postcss');
var cssnext = require('postcss-cssnext');
var cssnano = require('cssnano');
var browserify = require('browserify');
var source = require('vinyl-source-stream');
var buffer = require('vinyl-buffer');
var plumber = require('gulp-plumber'); // Added
```

With this addition, your `gulpfile` should look like the following screenshot:

Now that our plugin has been installed and included, let's add it as the first pipe within our `styles` task and remove the return from `gulp.src()`:

```
// Styles Task
gulp.task('styles', function () {
    gulp.src('app/css/*.css')
        .pipe(plumber())
        .pipe(concat('all.css'))
        .pipe(postcss([
            cssnext(),
            cssnano()
        ]))
        .pipe(gulp.dest('dist'));
});
```

Here is an example of what this looks like in our `gulpfile`:

In this example, it will keep `gulp.watch()` from crashing when it encounters an error and it will log error information to the console.

The only problem is that in many cases, you might not even realize an error has occurred. To remedy this, we can use an additional node module called `beeper` that will provide us with an audible alert when an error has occurred.

Installing beeper

As always, we must first install the plugin via npm:

```
npm install --save-dev beeper
```

The following screenshot reflects the command we will need to run to install the node module:

Including beeper

Once the plugin has been installed, we must add it to our list of requires to include it into our `gulpfile`. Refer to the following code snippet:

```
// Load Node Modules/Plugins
var gulp = require('gulp');
var concat = require('gulp-concat');
var uglify = require('gulp-uglify');
var jshint = require('gulp-jshint');
var imagemin = require('gulp-imagemin');
var connect = require('connect');
var serve = require('serve-static');
var browsersync = require('browser-sync');
var postcss = require('gulp-postcss');
```

```
var cssnext = require('postcss-cssnext');
var cssnano = require('cssnano');
var browserify = require('browserify');
var source = require('vinyl-source-stream');
var buffer = require('vinyl-buffer');
var plumber = require('gulp-plumber');
var beeper = require('beeper'); // Added
```

Writing an error helper function

Next, we will write a simple function that will act as our error handler. We can pass a reference to this function in a configuration object into `gulp-plumber` to customize how we are notified of errors:

```
// Error Handler
function onError(err) {
    beeper();
    console.log('Name:', err.name);
    console.log('Reason:', err.reason);
    console.log('File:', err.file);
    console.log('Line:', err.line);
    console.log('Column:', err.column);
}
```

The following screenshot shows what the error handler will look inside of our `gulpfile`:

When this function is executed, it will play a system sound to alert us using the beeper plugin and then log a few of the more important properties of the error object. Now, let's include it in the plumber() pipe as the value of the error handler property so that when gulp-plumber finds an error it will use our onError function instead of its default error handler:

```
// Styles Task
gulp.task('styles', function () {
    gulp.src('app/css/*.css')
        .pipe(plumber({
            errorHandler: onError
        }))
        .pipe(concat('all.css'))
        .pipe(postcss([
            cssnext(),
            cssnano()
        ]))
        .pipe(gulp.dest('dist'));
});
```

The following screenshot shows code for the styles task:

With this error handler is implemented, you now have full control over how your errors are reported, and thanks to `gulp-plumber`, we can handle those errors gracefully and Gulp will continue to watch for changes.

Source ordering

Another common issue that new Gulp users face is the way in which the files are ordered when they are processed. By default, each file in will be processed in order, based on its filename, unless specified otherwise. So, for example, when you are concatenating your CSS into a single file you will need to make sure that your normalized or reset styles are processed first.

To get around this, you can actually change the filenames of your source files by prepending numbers to them in the order that you would like them to be processed. So, for example, if you need a `normalize.css` file to render before an `abc.css` file, you can rename those files `1-normalize.css` and `2-abc.css`, respectively.

However, there are better ways to do this, and my personal favorite is to create an array at the beginning of the `gulpfile` so you can clearly order your files however you like. It's clean, simple, and easy to maintain.

Take the following code for example:

```
var cssFiles = ['assets/css/normalize.css', 'assets/css/abc.css'];

gulp.src('styles', function () {
    return gulp.src(cssFiles) // Pass in the array.
        .pipe(concat('site.css'))
        .pipe(gulp.dest('dist'));
});
```

But what if you have a large number of files and you only need to make sure that one of them is included first? Manually inserting every single one of those file paths into an array is not useful or easily maintainable, it's just time consuming and tedious.

The great news is that you can actually use globs in addition to explicit paths in your array. Gulp is smart enough to not process the same file twice. So, instead of specifying the order for every single file in the array, you can do something like this:

```
var cssFiles = ['assets/css/normalize.css', 'assets/css/*.css'];

gulp.src('styles', function () {
    return gulp.src(cssFiles) // Pass in the array.
        .pipe(concat('site.css'))
```

```
            .pipe(gulp.dest('dist'));
});
```

This will ensure that our `normalize.css` file is included first, and then it will include every other CSS file without including `normalize.css` twice in your concatenated code.

Clean task

Generating and processing files is great, but there may come a time when you or your teammates need to simply clear out the files that you have processed and start anew.

To do so, we are going to create another task that will clean out any processed files from our `dist` directory. To do this, we are going to use a node module called `del`, which will allow us to target multiple files and use globs in our file paths.

Installing the del module

Install the `del` module using npm and then save it to your list of development dependencies with the `--save-dev` flag:

```
npm install del --save-dev
```

The following screenshot shows the installation of the `del` module:

Including the del module

Once the module has been installed, you must add it to your list of required modules at the top of your `gulpfile`:

```
// Load Node Modules/Plugins
var gulp = require('gulp');
var concat = require('gulp-concat');
var uglify = require('gulp-uglify');
var jshint = require('gulp-jshint');
var imagemin = require('gulp-imagemin');
var connect = require('connect');
var serve = require('serve-static');
var browsersync = require('browser-sync');
var postcss = require('gulp-postcss');
var cssnext = require('postcss-cssnext');
var cssnano = require('cssnano');
var browserify = require('browserify');
var source = require('vinyl-source-stream');
var buffer = require('vinyl-buffer');
var plumber = require('gulp-plumber');
var beeper = require('beeper');
var del = require('del'); // Added
```

Writing a clean task

One way we can use this is by deleting an entire folder altogether. So, as an example, we could delete an entire folder, such as the `dist` directory, by creating a clean task:

```
gulp.task('clean', function () {
        return del(['dist']);
});
```

The following screenshot shows the newly created clean task in our `gulpfile`:

```
● ● ●                    ≡ gulpfile.js — ~/Development/gulp-book
gulpfile.js
                    .pipe(source( bundle.js ))
 87                 .pipe(buffer())
 88                 .pipe(gulp.dest('dist'));
 89         });
 90
 91         // Clean Task
 92         gulp.task('clean', function () {
 93             return del(['dist']);
 94         });
 95
 96         // Watch Task
 97         gulp.task('watch', function () {
 98             gulp.watch('app/css/*.css', ['styles', browsersync.reload]);
 99             gulp.watch('app/js/*.js', ['scripts', browsersync.reload]);
100             gulp.watch('app/img/*', ['images', browsersync.reload]);
101         });
102
103         // Default Task
104         gulp.task('default', ['styles', 'scripts', 'images', 'browsersync', 'watch']);
105
✓ No Issues  gulpfile.js  94:4                                    LF   UTF-8   JavaScript
```

Alternatively, we could use globs to select all of the files inside of the dist folder, but leave the dist folder itself intact:

```
gulp.task('clean', function () {
        return del(['dist/*']);
});
```

We could also delete all of our files inside the dist folder except a specific file, which we will leave untouched. We can accomplish this by prefixing the file path with an exclamation point, which is the logical *not* operator. Refer to the following code snippet:

```
gulp.task('clean', function () {
        return del(['dist/*', '!dist/site.css']);
});
```

External configuration

As you create or expand your gulpfile, you may reach a point where you would prefer to separate your configuration into an additional file. This is a common issue that arises as users get more comfortable with Gulp and wish to implement more control over how they configure their builds.

This can easily be done by creating an additional `config.json` file with each of the configuration options you would like to specify:

```
{
    "js": {
        "src": ["app/js/*.js"],
        "dest": "dist"
    },
    "css": {
        "src": ["app/css/*.css"],
        "dest": "dist"
    }
}
```

Then, we can include it in our `gulpfile` like all of our plugins and modules using a require function:

```
var config = require('./config.json');
```

The only difference with this `require` function is that you must prepend it with `./` to tell node that this file will reside in the main project directory instead of the `node_modules` directory, where all of the other installed plugins and modules reside.

Now, you can use this `config` in a number of ways to pass along the data inside it. You could simply access the information directly in any of your tasks.

The following code illustrates the use of the `config.json` that we created earlier in our styles task:

```
gulp.task('styles', function () {
    return gulp.src(config.css.src)
        .pipe(concat('site.css'))
        .pipe(myth())
        .pipe(gulp.dest(config.css.dest));
});
```

Task dependencies

When creating tasks, you might encounter a scenario in which you will need to ensure that a series of tasks run in a specific order.

As mentioned in the earlier chapters, the solution to this problem will differ based on which version of gulp you are using. Version 4.x introduces the `.series` method, which allows us to specify the order in which our tasks need to be executed directly whereas version 3.x requires us to specify the dependency in each of our task assignments.

To better understand this, take a look at an example using version 3.x.

For version 3.x, refer to the following code:

```
// Styles Task
gulp.task('styles', ['clean'], function () {
    gulp.src('app/css/*.css')
        .pipe(plumber({
        errorHandler: onError
    }))
    .pipe(concat('all.css'))
    .pipe(postcss([
        cssnext(),
        cssnano()
    ]))
    .pipe(gulp.dest('dist'));
});
```

As you can see in this example, we will provide the `clean` task dependency as the second argument of our task. This will ensure that clean is always run before the styles task, but it doesn't give us to ability to build out an execution order of many tasks.

Now, let's take a look at an example using version 4.x.

For version 4.x, refer to the following code:

```
// Watch Task
gulp.task('watch', function() {
    gulp.watch('app/css/*.css', gulp.series('clean', 'styles',
browsersync.reload));
    gulp.watch('app/js/*.js', gulp.series('clean', 'scripts',
browsersync.reload));
    gulp.watch('app/img/*', gulp.series('clean', 'images',
browsersync.reload));
});
```

In this example, you can see that instead of adding the dependency as an argument to our task directly, we can now leverage the `.series` method and specify an ordered execution chain of tasks.

Source maps

Minifying your JavaScript source code into distributable files can be a rough experience when it comes to debugging in the browser. Anytime you hit a snag and check your console for errors, you have to deal with compiled and unreadable code.

Modern browsers have some features that will make their best attempt to make the compiled code readable. However, this is usually still too unreadable to be practical and beneficial.

The solution to this problem is to generate source maps that will allow us to view the unbuilt versions of our code in the browser so that we can properly debug it.

Since we have already established a scripts task, you can simply add an additional plugin called `gulp-sourcemaps` that you can introduce into our pipechain, which will generate those source maps for us.

Installing a source maps plugin

To begin, we must first install the `gulp-sourcemaps` plugin:

```
npm install --save-dev gulp-sourcemaps
```

The following screenshot reflects the command to install the Gulp plugin:

```
✓ ~/Development/gulp-book
00:28 $ npm install --save-dev gulp-sourcemaps█
```

Including a source maps plugin

Once the plugin has been installed, we need to add it in our `gulpfile`:

```
// Load Node Modules/Plugins
var gulp = require('gulp');
var concat = require('gulp-concat');
var uglify = require('gulp-uglify');
var jshint = require('gulp-jshint');
var imagemin = require('gulp-imagemin');
var connect = require('connect');
var serve = require('serve-static');
var browsersync = require('browser-sync');
var postcss = require('gulp-postcss');
var cssnext = require('postcss-cssnext');
var cssnano = require('cssnano');
var browserify = require('browserify');
var source = require('vinyl-source-stream');
var buffer = require('vinyl-buffer');
var plumber = require('gulp-plumber');
var beeper = require('beeper');
var del = require('del');
var sourcemaps = require('gulp-sourcemaps'); // Added
```

The next screenshot reflects our required plugin:

Adding source maps to the task pipechain

Now that the plugin has been installed, you can jump back to the scripts task that you created in Chapter 2, *Performing Tasks with Gulp*, and fit the new plugin into the pipechain. Take a look at the following code snippet:

```
gulp.task('scripts', function() {
    return gulp.src('app/js/*.js')
        .pipe(sourcemaps.init()) // Added
        .pipe(jshint())
        .pipe(jshint.reporter('default'))
        .pipe(concat('all.js'))
        .pipe(uglify())
        .pipe(sourcemaps.write()) // Added
        .pipe(gulp.dest('dist'));
});
```

The following screenshot displays our modified pipechain:

In this code, we have added two lines. One has been added at the very beginning of the pipechain to initialize our source map plugin. The second has been added just before our pipe to Gulp's `dest()` method. This code will save our source maps inline with our compiled JavaScript file.

You can also save the source map as an additional file if you would prefer to keep your compiled code and your source maps separate. Instead of executing the `.write()` method without any arguments, you can pass in a path to instruct it to save your source map into a separate file:

```
gulp.task('scripts', function() {
    return gulp.src('app/js/*.js')
        .pipe(sourcemaps.init()) // Added
        .pipe(concat('all.js'))
        .pipe(jshint())
        .pipe(jshint.reporter('default'))
        .pipe(uglify())
        .pipe(sourcemaps.write('dist/maps')) // Added
        .pipe(gulp.dest('dist'));
});
```

Writing a gulpfile in ES2015

In the previous chapter, you learned how to use Babel to write our JavaScript code using features from ES2015. But, what about our gulpfile? It's JavaScript, so we should be capable of writing it in ES2015 for consistency, right? Of course we can! With a few minor changes, we can get our gulpfile running as we expect with all of the features of ES2015 with very little effort. Let's take a look.

Install node modules

First, we need to install a couple of node modules if they haven't been previously installed. If you are following along chronologically with the book, we will have already done this in the previous chapter. However, I'll just demonstrate how to install those plugins here for those who just need to revisit this tip later. Execute the following command to install babel modules:

```
npm install --save-dev babel-core babel-preset-env
```

The following screenshot reflects the command to install the babel modules:

```
✓ ~/Development/gulp-book
01:15 $ npm install --save-dev babel-core babel-preset-env
```

Adding .babelrc

The next step is to create a small file named .babelrc in the root directory of the project. Before we supplied this preset reference directly to the babelify transform in our Browserify task, this was just an alternative way to provide Babel with a configuration that works throughout our application. Inside of this file, we need to list the preset that we just installed as shown in the following code snippet:

```
{
    "presets": ["env"]
}
```

Renaming the gulpfile

Next, we need to rename `gulpfile.js` to `gulpfile.babel.js` so that it will trigger Babel to process the code inside of it. You can do this any way you like, but we're just going to do it inside of the command line since we're already using it:

```
mv gulpfile.js gulpfile.babel.js
```

The following screenshot demonstrates how to rename your `gulpfile` using the command line:

Update the gulpfile

Now, we can do the fun part and begin updating our `gulpfile`. We can now use all of the wonderful features that ES2015 gives us such as an updated import syntax, const/let keywords, and arrow functions to name a few. As a simple demonstration, we're just going to replace all of our current requires with the new import syntax and replace our task functions with arrow functions:

```
// Load Node Modules/Plugins
import gulp from 'gulp';
import concat from 'gulp-concat';
```

```
import uglify from 'gulp-uglify';
import jshint from 'gulp-jshint';
import imagemin from 'gulp-imagemin';
import connect from 'connect';
import serve from 'serve-static';
import browsersync from 'browser-sync';
import postcss from 'gulp-postcss';
import cssnext from 'postcss-cssnext';
import cssnano from 'cssnano';
import browserify from 'browserify';
import source from 'vinyl-source-stream';
import buffer from 'vinyl-buffer';
import plumber from 'gulp-plumber';
import beeper from 'beeper';
import del from 'del';
import sourcemaps from 'gulp-sourcemaps';

// Error Handler
function onError(err) {
    beeper();
    console.log('Name:', err.name);
    console.log('Reason:', err.reason);
    console.log('File:', err.file);
    console.log('Line:', err.line);
    console.log('Column:', err.column);
}

// Styles Task
gulp.task('styles', () => {
    gulp.src('app/css/*.css')
        .pipe(plumber({
            errorHandler: onError
        }))
        .pipe(concat('all.css'))
        .pipe(postcss([
            cssnext(),
            cssnano()
        ]))
        .pipe(gulp.dest('dist'));
});

// Scripts Task
gulp.task('scripts', () => {
    return gulp.src('app/js/*.js')
        .pipe(sourcemaps.init())
        .pipe(jshint())
        .pipe(jshint.reporter('default'))
        .pipe(concat('all.js'))
```

```
        .pipe(uglify())
        .pipe(sourcemaps.write())
        .pipe(gulp.dest('dist'));
});

// Images Task
gulp.task('images', () => {
    return gulp.src('app/img/*')
        .pipe(imagemin())
        .pipe(gulp.dest('dist/img'));
});

// Server Task
gulp.task('server', () => {
    return connect().use(serve(__dirname))
        .listen(8080)
        .on('listening', function() {
            console.log('Server Running: View at
http://localhost:8080');
        });
});

// BrowserSync Task
gulp.task('browsersync', () => {
    return browsersync({
            server: {
                baseDir: './'
            }
        });
});

// Browserify Task
gulp.task('browserify', () => {
    return browserify('./app/js/app.js')
        .transform('babelify', {
            presets: ['env']
        })
        .bundle()
        .pipe(source('bundle.js'))
        .pipe(buffer())
        .pipe(gulp.dest('dist'));
});

// Clean Task
gulp.task('clean', () => {
    return del(['dist']);
});
```

```
// Watch Task
gulp.task('watch', () => {
    gulp.watch('app/css/*.css', ['styles', browsersync.reload]);
    gulp.watch('app/js/*.js', ['scripts', browsersync.reload]);
    gulp.watch('app/img/*', ['images', browsersync.reload]);
});

// Default Task
gulp.task('default', ['styles', 'scripts', 'images', 'browsersync',
'watch']);
```

Summary

In this chapter, we discussed valuable tips and tricks to help resolve some common issues that users can run into while using Gulp. By implementing some additional Gulp plugins and node modules, we were able to make our tasks even more helpful and powerful.

We explored how to implement better error handling and prevented our watch task from silently exiting upon failure. Using arrays and external configs, we were able to gain more control over how our source files are processed, and how to prevent unnecessary repetition throughout our tasks.

Finally, we wrapped up this chapter by demonstrating how we can set tasks as dependencies, improve browser debugging with source maps, and a quick trick to enable us to write our gulpfile using ES2015.

Index

Printed in Great Britain
by Amazon